W9-AKC-484

Genetic Engineering

Other titles in the Issues in Focus *series:*

Genetic Engineering
Debating the Benefits and Concerns

Karen Judson

Enslow Publishers, Inc.

40 Industrial Road   PO Box 38
Box 398   Aldershot
Berkeley Heights, NJ 07922   Hants GU12 6BP
USA   UK

http://www.enslow.com

Copyright © 2001 by Karen Judson

Library of Congress Cataloging-in-Publication Data

Judson, Karen, 1941–
    Genetic engineering : debating the benefits and concerns /Karen
Judson
        p. cm. — (Issues in focus)
    Includes bibliographical references and index.
    ISBN 0-7660-1587-4
    1. Genetic engineering—Juvenile literature. [1. Genetic
engineering.] I. Title. II. Issues in focus (Hillside, N.J.)
    QH442 .J83   2001
    660.6'5—dc21
                                        00-011602
                                        CIP

Printed in the United States of America

10 9 8 7 6 5 4 3

To Our Readers: We have done our best to make sure all Internet
addresses in this book were active and appropriate when we went to
press. However, the author and the publisher have no control over and
assume no liability for the material available on those Internet sites or
on other Web sites they may link to. Any comments or suggestions can
be sent by e-mail to comments@enslow.com or to the address on the
back cover.

Illustration Credits: AMA Web site, p. 88; AP/World Wide
Photos, pp. 35, 61, 74; © Corel Corp., pp. 17, 28, 51, 105;
Enslow Publishers, Inc., pp. 20, 22, 24, 97, 107; © Susan
Dudley Gold, p. 78; © Jill K. Gregory, p. 57; Library of Congress,
pp. 46, 82; Photo Objects, p. 95; Robert Clink/University of
Pennsylvania Medical Center, p. 98.

Cover Illustration: AP/World Wide Photos.

Contents

1 Welcome to the Clone Age 7

2 Genetic Engineering 27

3 Gene Therapy 43

4 Genetic Testing 55

5 Genetic Discrimination, Privacy, and Civil Liberties 71

6 The Gene Business 84

7 Genetics in Our Future 100

Chapter Notes 113

Further Reading 120

Internet Addresses 122

Glossary 123

Index 126

1

Welcome to the Clone Age

"How far are we now from cloning humans?" was a question often asked after the February 1997 announcement of the birth of Dolly, a cloned Finn Dorset sheep. Dolly was born in July 1996 at the Roslin Institute near Edinburgh, Scotland. The announcement of her birth quickly spawned controversy because she was the world's first mammal cloned from an adult parent cell. That is, she was not the off-spring of a ram and a ewe, produced from the union of sperm and egg. Instead, Dolly was created from a cell scraped from the inside of her six-year-old mother's udder.

Dolly soon became the center of the

world's attention and the media closely followed her growth. Photographers exploding flashbulbs in her face made her so nervous her keepers limited visitors. A sweater knitted from her wool was placed on display in a museum. When Dolly gave birth to a baby named Bonnie in the spring of 1998, the event caused a media frenzy. Dolly had triplets in April 1999, and the news again made headlines: "Dolly Had Three Little Lambs."[1] Dolly's offspring were not clones. All were sired by a Welsh mountain ram named David. Although Dolly was a clone, she was exactly like her children born the natural way. All were normal, healthy sheep.

Many saw Dolly's arrival as proof that producing humans in the laboratory would be next. Soon after Dolly's birth, scientists announced the successful cloning of mice, cows, and pigs, but most scientists claimed that cloning humans was not likely to happen soon. Others, however, saw human cloning as inevitable.

"If it can be done, it will be done. And [human cloning] can be done," Eric Schon, a molecular biologist at Columbia University in New York, told reporters in August 2000. "The moment it could be done in sheep and mice and cows, it was only a matter of time for human cloning."[2]

What Is Cloning?

Clone comes from the Latin root meaning "to cut from." A clone is an organism grown from a single cell of the parent, and it is genetically identical to the parent. In other words, the genes and chromosomes found in each cell's nucleus are the same in clone and parent. Dolly is a clone. So is an identical twin. So are all the cells in our bodies, except for eggs and sperm.

The cloning method used to produce Dolly is called nuclear transfer. Scientists at the Roslin Institute first removed the nucleus, containing genes and chromosomes, from a sheep's unfertilized egg. They then inserted a cell from a second female sheep's udder into the egg. The udder cell, with nucleus and genetic material intact, was then fused with the egg cell by passing an electric pulse through the combined cells. The electric pulse caused changes in the unfertilized egg cell's outer membrane that tricked it into behaving as though it had been fertilized. The cell then began dividing, just as a fertilized egg would divide, and an embryo was formed.

It took many tries before the technique that produced Dolly was successful. At the Roslin Institute where Dolly was born, 277 eggs were mock-fertilized by nuclear transfer. Of the twenty-nine embryos that developed normally, thirteen were implanted in ewes.[3] One implantation resulted in a successful pregnancy, and Dolly was born.

The Cloning Controversy

If scientists could successfully clone sheep, people wondered if cloning humans could be far behind. This seemed a fearful prospect to many, and the possibility raised many ethical questions. Is it ethical (moral) for scientists to experiment with cloning humans? Should governments allow experiments in human cloning or should they pass laws against it?

After Dolly's birth, the governments of several countries took action to see that human cloning would not happen anytime soon. In 1998, thirteen European countries among the forty members of the Council of Europe signed the first international ban on human cloning. The agreement totally banned human cloning, but it allowed other animal cells to be cloned for research purposes. The thirteen countries who signed the agreement included Denmark, Finland, France, Greece, Iceland, Luxembourg, Norway, Portugal, Romania, San Marino, Spain, Sweden, and Turkey. Other Council of Europe member countries were expected to follow suit.[4]

In 1998, the government of the United Kingdom also said it objected to any research that might lead to "experimental" human beings. At the same time, the UK Department of Trade and Industry admitted that animal cloning research might someday offer "significant benefits" for human and animal health.[5]

In a landmark decision in August 2000, the UK government said that scientists should be allowed to clone human embryos for research. Legislation was to be introduced that would make human cloning legal under certain guidelines. If Parliament were to pass such legislation, the United Kingdom would become the first nation to legalize human cloning, if only for research. Scientists would be allowed to create early-stage embryos, called blastocysts, for research, but cloning humans for reproductive purposes would still be prohibited by British law.[6]

United States President Bill Clinton reacted to Dolly's birth by announcing that federal funds could not be used in efforts to clone humans. President Clinton had established the National Bioethics Advisory Committee by executive order in 1995. (Bioethics deals with the moral implications of medical decisions and scientific research.) The committee members advise the president and Congress on matters concerning genetics research. In 1998, the committee recommended that Congress pass a law making it illegal to clone humans. President Clinton proposed a law banning such research for five years.[7] Several measures to ban human cloning for reproductive purposes have been introduced in Congress, but, as of August 2000, none have passed.[8]

In January 1998 came an announcement that many had dreaded. Dr. Richard Seed, a Chicago physicist, declared that he would soon open a human cloning clinic, where he would clone babies for infertile couples. If barred from opening his clinic in the United States, Seed said he would go to Tijuana, Mexico, or to the Cayman Islands or the Bahamas. Seed planned to use the same cloning technique that produced Dolly. He claimed that he had assembled a group of doctors to work with him and had found four couples who were willing to be cloned.

In January 1998, a reporter for CNN asked about opposition to Seed's work. "There were an awful lot of people against the automobile, too," Seed replied. He claimed that any new technology passes through three phases. The first phase is fear and dread. The second phase is passivity and tolerance. The third phase is enthusiasm and acceptance. "That's what I think will happen with human cloning," Seed predicted.[9] In 2000, Seed's cloning clinic had not yet become a reality.

Why Experiment With Cloning?

Making babies is not the only purpose of human cloning. Another goal is the production of cells, tissues, and maybe even organs that could be used to help people with certain illnesses. The cloned cells, tissues, or organs would be transplanted, or surgically placed inside ill individuals, where scientists hope they can function normally and thus improve the patient's condition.

Cloning is an attractive prospect for transplants, because if a normal cell is taken from a patient and allowed to reproduce, the new cells can be transplanted within the same patient without fear of rejection. Rejection takes place when a patient's immune system produces special cells called antibodies that attack and destroy foreign tissue.

Stem cells are the key to cloning tissue for transplantation. Stem cells are the parent cells of all the body's different types of cells before they develop into blood cells, muscle cells, nerve cells, liver cells, and so on. Scientists have extracted stem cells from embryos and grown them in laboratories until they become differentiated into muscle cells or nerve cells. Scientists have also been able to make some adult cells turn from bone marrow cells into liver cells, a technique that is less controversial than using cells from embryos. This offers hope that specialized adult cells can be made to transform themselves into another type of cell, for repairing or improving the function of damaged tissue—without the fear of rejection.

Progress in Cloning Research

While governments rushed to ban human cloning, research in animal cloning moved forward:

- Two companies, Genzyme Transgenics Corporation and Advanced Cell Technology in Worcester, Massachusetts, announced in December 1997 that they would work together to produce cloned cattle embryos. Their goal was to produce animals with certain desirable characteristics, such as increased milk production.[10]

- In July 1998, a group of Japanese, American, and English scientists in Hawaii announced they had successfully cloned over fifty mice. They had even cloned clones from clones.[11] The research proved that scientists could clone identical animals to be used in experiments.

- In April 2000, scientists at Advanced Cell Technology, Inc., announced that cows they had cloned from a forty-five-day-old fetus may hold the secret to cell aging. The research has huge possibilities for treating age-related medical problems, said Michael West, president of the biotechnology company. "We could take one young cell from a patient and make hundreds or thousands of young cells and put them back in the patient and give them back a young immune system or give them back young cartilage in their knees."[12]

Dr. Robert P. Lanza, director of the study, added that, in the future, "If you had a damaged heart, we could take a few cells from you and grow up new heart cells and these would be your own cells so you wouldn't reject them." Of course there would probably be opposition to allowing this type of human cloning.[13]

Cloning Methods

There are several ways of cloning cells in the laboratory, in addition to nuclear transfer, which was the method used to create Dolly. Other techniques include molecular cloning, cellular cloning, and splitting embryos.

Molecular cloning is useful in producing small segments of genetic material that can be snipped from cells and inserted in other cells. A few molecules are cut from a chromosome of one cell and put into a second cell. The altered cell then reproduces or clones itself. The new cells have different genetic material than the original, unaltered cell.

Cellular cloning takes place naturally every minute in our bodies, as when dead skin cells are replaced by new skin cells. Cellular cloning is also accomplished in the laboratory.

Embryo splitting and nuclear transfer are the two cloning methods most often used to clone entire animals. Nuclear transfer is explained above. When scientists split embryos, they first fertilize an animal's egg in the laboratory. They then split the early embryo into sections of a few cells each. The small sections of cells are implanted in the wombs of female animals. In this manner, several animals are cloned from one fertilized egg. To date, cattle, sheep, and mice have most often been cloned in this manner.

Frequently Asked Questions About Cloning

As news of Dolly's unusual birth spread, so, too, did concern over cloning possibilities. A few frequently asked questions were answered online by *New Scientist* magazine in their "Cloning Special Report."[14] Answers are paraphrased below:

- Is cloning an unnatural process?

- No, because many simple organisms in nature, such as bacteria and yeast, reproduce by cloning a parent cell. Some larger organisms, such as shrimp called Artemia perthenogenetica and small insects called aphids also reproduce by cloning. And, again, identical twins are clones.

- If human cloning is perfected, could a mad scientist someday clone a series of Adolf Hitlers?

- This is highly unlikely, because to clone Adolf Hitler, scientists would need living or frozen cells from his body, which are not available.

- Could scientists eventually produce clones to be used for replacement body organs?

- In theory, yes, but because of the legal, social, religious, and moral issues involved, it is unlikely that an entire human being would ever be cloned for use solely as "spare parts." It has been suggested, however, that scientists might someday clone individual organs, such as livers or kidneys, to be used for transplant purposes.

Genetic Material in Cells

Genetics, including cloning, can be better understood by grasping a few simple facts about cells. Cells are the microscopic units that make up all organisms. Each cell consists of a jelly-like substance called cytoplasm and a dense, centrally located structure called a nucleus. An outer cell membrane encloses the cytoplasm and the nucleus. The nucleus has its own outer membrane. The nucleus contains all of a cell's chromosomes and genes. Genes are microscopic nodes found on chromosomes. Genes trigger the expression of all of an organism's traits. In humans, genes are responsible for eye and hair color, height, skin color, and every other characteristic.

Chromosomes are composed of large molecules of deoxyribonucleic acid (DNA). The DNA molecule is shaped like a long, twisting staircase or ladder. The shape is called a double helix and is much like a stepladder with side slats that have been twisted by a strong wind.

The composition of DNA explains its shape. DNA is formed from units called nucleotides. Each nucleotide is a molecule made up of three parts. One part is a sugar called deoxyribone. The second part is

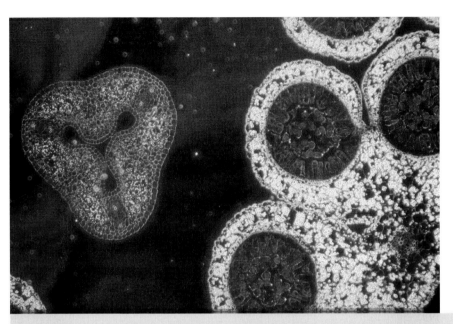

The secret of life stems from the tiny cell. The nucleus of a cell contains all the chromosomes and genes that result in the creation of a living organism.

a phosphate group. Nitrogen-containing bases make up the third part of the nucleotide molecule. The outer slats of the DNA double helix are sugar-phosphate supports that twist around. The inner steps of the ladder are paired nitrogen-containing bases. The bases are held together by hydrogen bonds. The four organic bases found in the DNA molecule are adenine (A), thymine (T), guanine (G) and cytosine (C). The bases comprise the genes.

Because the same four bases, A, T, G, and C, make up DNA molecules in all organisms, scientists can swap DNA from one organism to another. This process is called genetic engineering. Therefore, for example, a bacteria, virus, yeast, or plant cell can be made to accept human or animal DNA.

The universal composition of DNA has led to some unusual combinations. For instance, in 1986, a Japanese scientist took the gene for luciferase protein from a firefly and put it into tobacco plant cells. Luciferase acts on a chemical produced by fireflies called luciferin, to make them glow. When the scientist gave luciferin to the genetically engineered tobacco plants, they glowed in the dark.[15]

The Inheritance of Genetic Material

Chromosomes are found in pairs inside an organism's cell nuclei, because every organism inherits one set of chromosomes from each parent. The number of paired chromosomes is different for each kind of plant and animal. Humans have twenty-three pairs of chromosomes, sheep have twenty-six, and mice have twenty. In humans, twenty-three chromosomes are inherited from the father and twenty-three are inherited from the mother, for a total of forty-six.

Reproductive cells are the only cells that contain just half of an organism's complete number of chromosomes. Human reproductive cells, called gametes, are the eggs produced by females and the sperm produced by males. Human egg cells and sperm cells have twenty-three chromosomes each. When male and female gametes unite, they form one fertilized cell with forty-six chromosomes. Soon after fertilization, cell division begins. Cell division continues until the embryo becomes a fetus inside the mother's womb, and, finally, a baby is born.

In this manner—sperm fertilizing egg—the chromosomes inside the cells' nuclei are passed from parents to offspring. Again, twenty-three chromosomes come from the mother and twenty-three come from the father. Since genes for specific traits or characteristics are located on the chromosomes, the genetic material passed on by parents is responsible for all inherited traits that appear in the offspring.

Dolly's chromosome composition differs from the norm in that the udder cell that produced her came from a female sheep and did not involve union of egg and sperm. Therefore, all of her chromosomes came from her mother alone. This meant that Dolly was a genetic twin, or clone, of her mother.

The Father of Genetics

Most of what we know about genetics, including cloning, can be traced back to Gregor Mendel, a Czech monk who is called the father of modern genetics. Mendel studied heredity by growing pea plants. From 1856 to 1864 he grew at least twenty-eight thousand peas in his monastery garden in Brno, Czechoslovakia. Mendel crossed pea plants with different characteristics, such as red flowers and white flowers, by placing pollen from one plant on the flower pistils of another plant. After pollination, the fertilized ovules became seeds that Mendel planted so that he could study the offspring of the pea plants.

From his experiments, Mendel correctly concluded that each male or female parent plant must have two factors that define a characteristic, such as flower color or plant height. One factor is inherited from the father and one from the mother. When sex cells form, the factors are split. The result is that parents pass on one factor for each characteristic to their off-spring. Each offspring receives a complement of

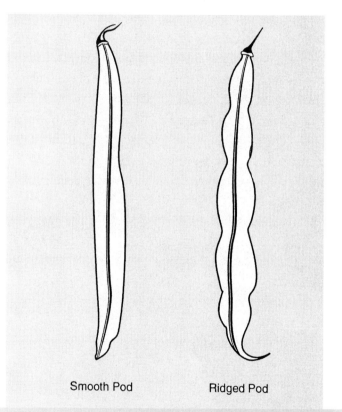

Smooth Pod   Ridged Pod

Most of what we know about heredity can be traced to a nineteenth century Czech monk named Gregor Mendel. Mendel studied heredity by growing pea plants.

factors from the father and a complement from the mother.

Mendel also determined that when a factor for a certain trait such as red flowers is dominant, that trait will appear in the offspring in higher numbers. Recessive traits, such as white flowers, are not expressed when a dominant factor is present. Therefore, unless both parents carry only the recessive genes for a trait, recessive traits usually show up in fewer numbers in the offspring.

Mendel found that when a gene for a dominant trait and a recessive gene for the same trait (as in flower color) were present in the same parent plant, the dominant trait was usually expressed in the offspring. The recessive trait sometimes showed up in the offspring, however, depending on the genetic makeup of both parents. For example, sometimes when Mendel crossed two red-flowered peas, white-flowered peas also showed up in the offspring. The ratio of red to white offspring in such a cross was three red to one white. The genetic makeup of both parents in such a cross would look like this, with R the dominant gene for red flowers and r the recessive gene for white flowers:

Rr x Rr = RR, Rr, and rr

Two red-flowered plants could produce all red-flowered offspring, if both parent plants carried only the dominant genes for red:

RR x RR = RR

Crossing two white-flowered peas would result in all white offspring, because only recessive genes are present:

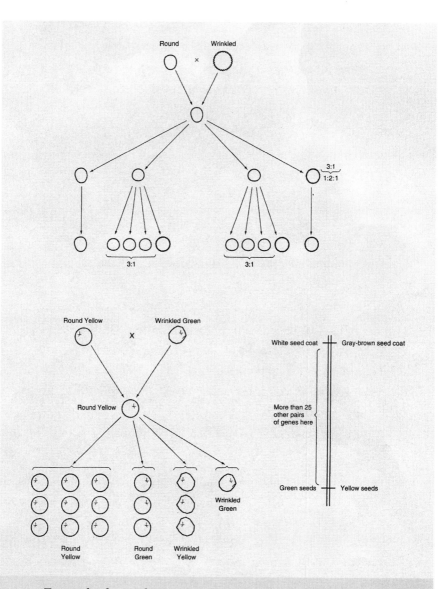

To study how characteristics are passed down through generations, Gregor Mendel crossed pea plants with different characteristics. So, for example, he crossed round yellow and green peas with wrinkled peas to discover what would result.

rr x rr = rr

Mendel's factors were later called "genes," from the Greek word meaning "to give birth to." Today we know that genes allow parent organisms to pass characteristics on to their offspring. Chromosomes and genes also tell organisms how to duplicate themselves.

Mutations

We also know that sometimes genes can change, so that the expected trait is altered. These changes in genes are called mutations. Mutations can just occur for no obvious reason. The odds for that happening, however, are about one in fifty thousand.[16] More often, gene mutations are the result of exposure to an outside source, such as certain chemicals, radiation, or other factors that have not yet been identified. The substances that we know to cause gene mutations, such as radiation, alcohol and other drugs, and even sunlight, are called mutagens.

Each of us inherits hundreds of genetic mutations from our parents. In addition, our own DNA can undergo some thirty new mutations during our lifetime.[17] Some mutations are harmless, and their effects are never noticed in offspring. Most mutations, however, are not beneficial. Many cause diseases or malfunctions when they are inherited by offspring. These hereditary conditions are passed on through successive generations. Since most mutated genes are recessive, we must inherit the same recessive gene from each parent for the trait it represents

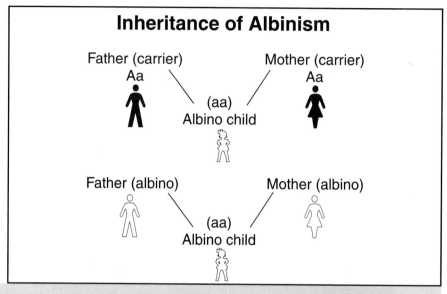

Inheritance of Albinism

Father (carrier)
Aa

Mother (carrier)
Aa

(aa)
Albino child

Father (albino)

Mother (albino)

(aa)
Albino child

To produce an albino child, the parents must be albinos, or both must have genes for albinism. If the parents are carriers, they can also produce children who are not albino.

to be expressed. (Except in the case of sex-linked recessive genes, which are discussed in Chapter 4.)

Genetic Research Leads to Genetic Engineering

Mendel's work laid the groundwork for all future research in genetics. As shown by Dolly's birth, scientists now have the technology to clone life. Today's genetic researchers also have the ability to change an organism's complement of genes. Through a process called genetic engineering, scientists can rearrange the genetic material in an organism's cells. For example, they can splice genetic material from plants, animals, or bacteria into the DNA of other organisms. DNA that is manipulated in this manner is called recombinant DNA. Genetically engineered plants and animals are said to be bioengineered. Genetic engineering and recombinant DNA technology are called biotechnology.

Genetics in Your Life

People are concerned about genetic research because genetics affects our lives in many ways. Why does a daughter inherit a mother's curly red hair and green eyes, instead of her father's straight blond hair and blue eyes? Sometimes there are hereditary diseases in a family, such as sickle cell anemia or hemophilia, that a child may be at risk of developing. A person might pass on his or her musical talent or math ability to a son or daughter. Having grandparents who live well into their eighties may mean that grandchildren will also live long lives.

Armed with some knowledge of genetics, people can answer some of the questions they have about their own heredity. A basic knowledge of genetics makes it easier to follow the media reports about scientific research, without the fear that comes from ignorance. That knowledge allows a person to form educated opinions on the questions raised and make informed decisions when genetics issues closely affect one's life.

Clearly, the issues surrounding genetics research extend far beyond an individual's family inheritance. There are many practical and ethical considerations associated with genetics research that often are difficult for non-scientists to understand. As with any difficult subject, however, if basic facts are mastered, we are better able to make sense of both sides of an issue. And there are definitely two opposing sides concerning genetics research.

Some scientists predict that genetic research can give us improved crops to help relieve world hunger. Or the chance to wipe out some of the most harmful genetic diseases. But progress in genetics research has also raised some frightening questions. For instance, if scientists can manipulate genes and chromosomes, what kind of world will we inhabit in the twenty-first century? Will parents be able to choose the characteristics, such as gender, height, and eye and hair color, of babies they bring into the world? If human cloning is allowed, will governments create a warrior race to fight wars or police cities? Will human beings be cloned as workers for specific occupations? And, a question closer to the present: Will our genetic history be available to schools, prospective employers, or others who have an interest, such as insurance carriers?

To put to rest some of the fears listed above, responsible scientists list four main reasons for pursuing biotechnology development: better health, better food, an improved environment, and better business. There are those who agree that biotechnology can fulfill the promise of better lives and a better world. And, of course, there are those who argue that the opposite is true. This book presents facts from both sides of the argument, in order to help readers become more informed about genetics research and how it can affect each life now and in the future.

2

Genetic Engineering

In James Patterson's novel, *When The Wind Blows*, evil scientists cross human embryos with bird embryos to create children who have beautifully feathered wings and can fly. They also have dangerously fast metabolic rates, enlarged chest cavities, and arms and hands unlike most children.[1] The plot is pure fiction, of course, but some people fear that such scary scenarios are possible through genetic engineering.

Old and New Biotechnology

Long before advances in genetic engineering research would inspire a plot like

27

Patterson's, Gregor Mendel's genetics work led to selective breeding. Selective breeding involves breeding plants and animals for genes that control certain desirable characteristics in the offspring. For example, several years ago two strains of corn—one tasty and one resistant to disease—were combined through cross-pollination to produce corn that has both characteristics. Selective breeding is sometimes called old biotechnology.

Selective breeding has been practiced for centuries. It has produced corn from maize, thoroughbreds from wild horses, and cows that give

Gregor Mendel's early work in genetics led to a practice called selective breeding. For example, the many different kinds of dogs that now exist were bred from wolves.

more milk. The many different breeds of dogs, bred originally from wolves, are also the result of selective breeding. (Some argue that selective breeding of dogs has perhaps not always been helpful to the animals, considering the back problems of dachshunds, hip deformities in Labrador retrievers, or the tendency toward cancer in boxers.)

Scientists still use selective breeding to preserve or achieve desirable traits in a species. For example, at the University of California, Irvine, evolutionary biologist Michael Rose is studying aging by breeding fruit flies. Fruit flies are often used in genetics research because they reproduce every fourteen days and have just four pairs of chromosomes. Rose found that female flies which reproduce at a young age die early. He found that he could keep the female flies alive longer by removing their developing eggs. And when Rose allowed the females to reproduce at an older age, their offspring also lived longer.[2]

One disadvantage of selective breeding is that it is slow. It takes many generations, over time, to achieve results. And selective breeding does not allow for transference of specific genes. For example, an early-maturing peach was developed through selective breeding, but other genes in the plant's makeup caused the fruit to break open on the tree. Through genetic engineering, perhaps a gene could have been introduced that would allow the early-maturing peach to remain on the tree until picked, without breaking open.

Instead of waiting for several generations of off-spring to mature and reproduce, scientists can use genetic engineering. It allows scientists to transfer genes for desirable characteristics from one organism to another. It also allows for selecting specific genes in combinations that would not be possible through selective breeding. For example, strawberries frost easily, which makes them hard to grow in some climates. A few years ago, however, researchers discovered that a fish called the Arctic flounder produces its own chemical antifreeze to protect itself in cold Arctic waters. Research was then begun to introduce the anti-freeze gene into fruits and vegetables like strawberries and soy beans to make them more frost resistant.[3]

Agricultural Biotechnology

Like selective breeding, agricultural biotechnology has been practiced for many years. Agricultural biotechnology involves the transfer of genes from a plant or animal to another plant. Researchers are trying to make crops easier and less costly for farmers to grow, improve crop yield, and create healthier fruits and vegetables that are more attractive to consumers. Results already realized include:

- hardier crops that survive in extreme temperatures or environments

- soybeans and corn that are resistant to pests, fungus, and other diseases, and yield more produce per acre

- wheat with more fiber

- beta-carotene enriched "golden rice" that can

keep as many as 250 million children worldwide from going blind. The beta-carotene is converted to vitamin A in the body, and vitamin A is vital for healthy vision[4]

- tomatoes with more beta-carotene, a longer shelf life in stores, and a richer flavor

In 1999, the U.S. Department of Agriculture estimated that genetically engineered crops made up 35 percent of corn and 55 percent of soybeans and occupied 25 percent of crop land in the United States. That same year, the Organic Consumers Union listed thirty-six genetically modified vegetables and fruits on the market.[5]

On the agenda for the future are crops that:

- prevent iron-deficiency anemia (a variation of the golden rice mentioned above)

- lower cholesterol

- help prevent cancer

- produce biodegradable plastic[6]

Also in development are bananas that produce an antigen against hepatitis B, a serious liver disease; apples that do not turn brown when you cut or bite into them; and onions that do not make your eyes water.[7]

Many farmers and agribusinesses see long-range benefits to planting genetically modified crops, including, of course, increased profits. Therefore, such crops have come into widespread use in the United States since 1996.[8] There are two opposing sides to the issue. Here are a few of the arguments most often used for and against the use of genetically modified food:

For: Improved nutritional value, as in the examples listed above.

Against: Altered nutritional value is not always good. For example, in one experiment, a gene from a Brazil nut was inserted into soybean cells for improved nutritional value. Instead of improving nutrition, however, the protein produced by the Brazil nut gene was the one responsible for the allergic reaction to Brazil nuts. This allergic trait was passed to the soybeans. The soybeans could have caused allergic reactions in millions of unsuspecting consumers, so they were not put on the market.[9]

For: Less need for chemical weed killers, pesticides, and fertilizers, since many genetically altered crops are naturally pest and disease resistant without the help of chemicals. As farmers are able to reduce their uses of chemicals, they help the environment.

Against: Pests and diseases can develop a tolerance to the genetically engineered resistance factors in the crop. (But, argues the other side, plant pests and diseases can also develop a tolerance to chemical pesticides, which environmentalists also condemn.) This could result in super strains of pests and diseases and increased use of chemicals to control them.

Another argument is that genetically modified crops that are weed resistant may interbreed with closely related weed plants. If this happens, the new breed of weeds may be difficult or impossible to control with known herbicides. Also, the genetically modified crop itself could become a noxious weed if it grows outside prescribed areas. And they might cross-pollinate with natural plants that could harm insects and birds that eat them.[10]

For: The technology has been thoroughly tested and examined, so that the crops produced through genetic engineering are safe to grow and to eat.

Against: In order to rush their products to market, companies have not adequately tested and examined genetically modified crops.

Countries Reach Agreement About Genetically Modified Crops

Because some countries will not import genetically modified foods, the subject has been hotly debated at world trade conferences. In a January 2000 agreement, in Montreal, Canada, more than 130 countries agreed to regulate trade in genetically modified organisms (GMOs). The United Nations-sponsored agreement addresses concerns of European countries that import genetically modified foods, and of the two major export countries, Canada and the United States. When all 130 nations ratify the agreement, shipments containing GMOs will have to be labeled appropriately. The agreement also protects the right of countries to close their markets to genetically modified crops, even without scientific evidence that the product is harmful.[11]

Animal Biotechnology

Animal biotechnology involves manipulating the genetic material of animals. A type of animal biotechnology called transgenics refers to combining the genetic material of two or more different animals. It can also involve adding plant DNA to animal cells. A second type of animal biotechnology, called xenotransplantation, refers to the use of animal organs or tissue in humans. Many critics of agricultural biotechnology object to transgenics and xenotransplantation.

On Halloween, 1999, anti-genetic-engineering activists who feared xenotransplantation marched in New York City and Washington, D.C. to protest what they called "Frankenscence." Costumed marchers wore pig snouts, carried models of a pig-human cross, and danced with signs warning that the use of animal organs in humans could transfer deadly animal viruses to people.

Alix Fano, organizer of the march, said Halloween costumes were appropriate because "it's a very ghoulish technology, in our opinion." Similarly, Halloween marchers in Washington, D.C. who were protesting transgenics wore Frankenstein masks to a local Safeway grocery store. The group made a monster they called the "Gene Beast"—a creature with a strawberry head combined with a fish.[12]

Xenotransplantation

Despite disagreement about mixing animal and human DNA, however, research in this area has continued. For instance, scientists researching xenotransplantation have long tried to use animal organs and tissues to treat human ailments, but, until recently, with little success. The main problem has

Protests against genetically altered foods have been widespread worldwide. In this Boston protest, marchers carried a mock-up of a coffin. The demonstrators believe that genetically engineered food and medicine have not been proved safe and should not be sold.

been that the immune response triggered in human patients tends to quickly destroy transplanted animal organs and tissues. The immune response is the body's reaction to foreign tissue. Antibodies are produced that defend the body by destroying tissue not recognized as the body's own.

Recently, however, drugs that suppress the immune reaction have allowed physicians to use pig tissues, including heart valves, clotting factors, islet cells, brain cells, and skin, to treat human ailments. Now there is hope that genetically altered pigs can eventually provide entire organs for ailing people without fear of an immune reaction. At least two companies are injecting human genes into one- and two-cell pig embryos. The object is to produce an animal that makes the protective protein found in human blood that keeps humans from rejecting transplanted human organs.[13]

Pigs are more likely than any other animal to be used as donors because they are easily bred, and because they closely resemble humans in weight and physiology. In 1996, the liver of one such genetically altered pig kept seventeen-year-old Robert Pennington alive for several hours while doctors located a human donor liver to replace his dying organ. Surgeons placed the pig liver in a saline bath next to Robert, then cycled the boy's blood through the pig's organ. The pig's organ temporarily took over the duties of cleansing Pennington's blood that his own organ could no longer perform, until a human donor liver could be found.

"We could tell right away that [the pig's liver]

was working," Pennington's grandmother told a reporter for *Newsweek*. "The blood leaving Robert's body was grayish, but it looked normal as it went back in."[14]

Pennington soon received a human donor liver, and the temporary help of the pig liver was no longer needed. He survived his transplantation surgery and in January 2000, at age twenty, was planning to start an Internet business.[15]

Much of the research in animal biotechnology concerns aging. At Southern Methodist University in Dallas, for example, Raj Sohal, a professor of biology, is studying the effects of oxygen free radicals on the aging of animal cells. Free radicals are molecules that have lost one of two electrons normally present. This makes them highly reactive. They bounce around, trying to pair with other electrons, and in the process they damage proteins, fats, and DNA in cells. Some enzymes eventually combine with the free radicals, turning them into water, but by that time the damage has been done. "Oxygen is a paradoxical substance," Sohal said. "On the one hand, it gives us life. It is also very dangerous because its use necessarily involves the generation of free radicals, which are slowly killing us. Living and dying are part of the same coin."[16]

In his experiments, Sohal isolated the gene that prevents the formation of free radicals and inserted it into fruit fly embryos. The result was a fruit fly that lived 30 percent longer than normal flies. The value of Sohal's experiments is that he may have found one way to prevent cells from aging. Perhaps soon scientists will be able to prolong life by turning off free-radical-causing genes in human cells.[17]

On the other hand, perhaps turning off free-radical-causing genes in human cells will have unpredictable adverse effects, due to the complexity of gene action and our limited understanding of it. The only way to find out for sure is through research.

Despite the objections of animal-rights activists, research in animal biotechnology has progressed at a rapid rate. For instance, in an example that could have been taken from a science fiction novel, a company in Canada announced in May 2000 that they had combined spider DNA and goat DNA. Scientists at the Quebec, Canada-based Nexia Biotechnologies company said their goal was to produce a material so strong that it can be used in antimissile defense systems, ultralight bullet-resistant vests, and medical suture thread. Nanny goats bred from two bioengineered male goats will be able to produce milk with tough protein fibers, because of the spider DNA in their genetic makeup. A super-strong material, called BioSteel, will be manufactured from the protein in the goats' milk. Nexia spokesperson Jeffrey Turner said that the milk produced by one goat in one month could make one bullet-resistant vest. Cycling spider DNA through the goats lets the company take advantage of the strength and elasticity of spider silk without the impossible task of raising millions of spiders. Production was scheduled to begin late in the year 2000.[18]

Evidence Both Pro and Con

People on both sides of the genetic engineering debate have strong opinions. Those in favor of genetic engineering see boundless opportunities for good, but critics are perhaps more cautious and see the possibility for catastrophe, as well as good. For instance, Cornell University researchers released a study in May 1999 that seemed to validate environmentalists' worst fears. The study tested a corn called Bt that had been genetically altered to produce a toxin that would kill a caterpillar called the European corn borer. The researchers wanted to see if the corn's pollen might also kill the caterpillars of monarch butterflies. Monarch caterpillars feed almost exclusively on milkweed plants, so the Cornell researchers dusted milkweed plants with pollen from Bt, the genetically modified corn. They dusted a second group of milkweed plants with pollen from normal corn. Then they observed monarch caterpillars feeding on both groups of plants. The research team reported that 44 percent of the monarch caterpillars that ate leaves covered with Bt pollen died after four days. Caterpillars remained healthy when they ate leaves coated with pollen from normal corn. The study found no evidence that monarch caterpillars were dying from ingesting Bt corn pollen in the wild. Still, biotech protestors feared that the corn could kill monarchs and all the birds and small mammals that eat them.

"This is a warning that we may have more of a problem than the [agricultural biotechnology] industry would have us believe," said Jane Rissler of the Union of Concerned Scientists in a May 1999 issue of *USA Today.*[19]

After the Cornell report, a group of biotechnology and pesticide companies funded several studies to see if Bt corn actually poses a threat to monarch butterflies. In November 1999, results of these studies were released. Findings from several studies in Maryland, Pennsylvania, Iowa, and Ontario suggested that pollen from Bt corn posed little, if any, threat to the butterflies. Windblown pollen seldom left cornfields, the researchers claimed. And when it did, it was not present in amounts large enough to kill caterpillars. Iowa State University's John Pleasant said that monarchs may be threatened under some conditions, but in general, are probably "100 percent safe."[20]

The two studies yielding opposite results illustrate the difficulty of reconciling the two sides of the genetic engineering argument. Education and thoughtful debate are the key, with both sides willing to learn and to consider differing opinions.

Ethical Issues

Now that genes can be transferred from one organism to another, many ethical questions have arisen. For example, when dedicated vegetarians eat strawberries, should they be concerned to learn that the fruit contains DNA from a fish, thus defeating their attempts to avoid all animal flesh and products in their diets? If pigs and cattle contain human genes, is the person who eats the meat a cannibal? Scientists debating these questions explain that DNA is, structurally, the same, whether it is taken from a strawberry, fish, bacteria, or a person. It is the unique arrangement of the genes within the chromosomes that determines whether an organism is plant or animal, strawberry or fish. Therefore, they counsel, the above questions are meaningless if one considers only the structure of the DNA used.

On the other hand, people who consider the questions emotionally, rather than scientifically, may continue to feel squeamish or outraged. The difficult questions may never be answered to everyone's complete satisfaction, but if genetic engineering is to realize its potential for good, scientists and consumers will need to find common ground.

Today's responsible scientists know that many people fear genetic engineering because of the possible harmful effects and misuse. W. French Anderson, professor of biochemistry and pediatrics at the University of Southern California Keck School of Medicine, is a pioneer in the field of human genetic engineering. He hopes that genetic engineering will allow people to lead healthier, happier, and longer lives, but he also cautions about dangers. "Once we have the ability to give a patient any gene we want in order to treat a disease," he wrote in the January 1, 2000, issue of *Newsweek*, "then we will also have the ability to give a human being genes for any purpose besides therapy." This, says Anderson, could lead to the creation of "designer" human beings and permanent changes in the human gene pool.

"Our only protection is to accept clear stopping points," Anderson continues. "And the only way to achieve those is to make sure that society is informed and can recognize the dangers and prevent misuses before it is too late."[21]

Most responsible scientists and those on both sides of the argument agree that the best protection against possible abuses of genetic engineering is an informed society. It is also important that guidelines for genetic research and therapy be accepted that put the welfare of each individual first.

3

Gene Therapy

People have always gossiped about celebrities and royalty. Today we can get the latest gossip about almost any movie or rock star, or about royal families around the world simply by turning on the television or buying a newspaper. In nineteenth century England, however, most gossip spread by word of mouth. One of the juiciest stories at that time was about the "curse of the Coburgs" that had been cast upon Queen Victoria's royal family.

Queen Victoria, Princess of Saxe-Coburg before her marriage, was the reigning monarch in Great Britain from 1837 to 1901. Victoria married her first cousin, Albert, in 1840. Of the nine children born to Victoria and Albert, one had hemophilia. Hemophilia causes those who have the disease to bleed easily, due to lack of a clotting factor that is present in normal blood. Blood clotting factors stop bleeding in normal individuals. The Queen's eighth child, Prince Leopold, Duke of Albany, was the only one of her four sons to inherit the disease. As a boy, Prince Leopold could not run and play with the other children because he bruised easily and suffered severe hemorrhages. Queen Victoria protected him, but Prince Leopold died at the age of thirty-one after a minor fall.

According to the Coburg legend, the curse that caused Prince Leopold's disease dated from the early 1800s when a Coburg prince married Antoinette de Kohary, a Hungarian princess. The story said that a monk was jealous of the wealthy couple and cursed future generations of Coburgs with the disease.

A curse made just as much sense as anything else to explain hemophilia in Queen Victoria's time, because no one then knew about genes and chromosomes. Today, we know that hemophilia is caused by a gene passed from mother to son on the X chromosome. The fact that the gene is transmitted on the X chromosome makes hemophilia a sex-linked disease. We also know that the hemophilia gene probably originated as a mutation in Queen Victoria or in one of her ancestors.

Studying the way hemophilia is inherited has helped scientists reach this conclusion. We now know that the recessive gene for hemophilia is carried on the X chromosome. (Remember—traits caused by recessive genes are not expressed if the dominant gene for the trait is also present.) The X and Y chromosomes are sex-determining chromosomes. Two X chromosomes produce a girl, and an X and a Y chromosome produce a boy. Since boys inherit just one X chromosome and girls inherit two, sons are more likely to inherit the gene for hemophilia if it is present in the mother or father. Daughters can be carriers, but they inherit the disease only if both parents carry the recessive gene. In girls born with hemophilia, the fathers have hemophilia. The mothers also either have the disease or have normal blood but carry the gene for hemophilia.

The hemophilia gene was passed on to future generations of Victoria's family when her sons and daughters married and had children. When Victoria died in 1901, she had forty grandchildren. Her descendants married into almost every royal family of Europe, thus spreading the disease.

Gene Therapy

Today scientists are experimenting with gene therapy as a way to permanently help people who have hemophilia and other inherited diseases. Gene therapy involves inserting healthy genes into human cells to correct or prevent diseases. When genes are introduced into body cells other than eggs and sperm, this is called somatic cell gene therapy. Any effects are limited to the person receiving the therapy as the new genes are not passed on to future generations.

An entire era—the Victorian Age—is named after Queen Victoria, who ruled Great Britain for most of the nineteenth century. Lesser known is that Queen Victoria and Prince Albert had a son, Prince Leopold, with hemophilia.

Germ line gene therapy refers to the correction of a genetic problem in an individual's eggs or sperm. This means that once a problem such as hemophilia is corrected inside the reproductive cells, it cannot be passed on to offspring.

In addition to hemophilia, gene therapy trials have been conducted on people with muscular dystrophy, cystic fibrosis, HIV infection, rheumatoid arthritis, acute hepatic failure, many forms of cancer, a rare enzyme disorder called ADA deficiency, and other diseases. To date gene therapy is still in its infancy.

The Bubble Boy

David Vetter was born in 1972 with a rare inherited disorder called severe combined immune deficiency (SCID). David lacked a key immune system gene, which meant that his immune system did not function. Normally, the body's immune system attacks foreign invaders, such as bacteria or viruses, and destroys them. Because every bacterium, virus, and speck of dust could cause a life-threatening illness for David, he lived his entire life inside a germ-free plastic bubble.[1] David, nicknamed "the bubble boy," once said that his dream was "to walk barefoot in the grass,"[2] but he died in 1984 at age twelve before he could realize his dream.

One Success Story

If David Vetter had been born more recently, chances are that today he would be living a normal life. As reported by French researchers in *Science*, two infants born with SCID were successfully treated with gene therapy at the Hospital Necker-Enfants Malades in Paris in 1999. The scientists removed bone marrow from the infants and inserted a normal copy of the missing immune system gene into the bone marrow cells. The bioengineered cells were then returned to the infants' bodies. The new genes worked as they should, and after ten months of follow-up, the infants had developed normal immune systems. The children are expected to live normal lives.[3]

Gene therapy shows great medical promise, but it experienced a setback in September 1999 when eighteen-year-old Jesse Gelsinger died. Gelsinger had an inherited liver disorder called ornithine transcarbamylase deficiency (OTC). The disease prevents the body from processing nitrogen which leads to a buildup of toxic substances in the body that can be fatal. As part of a gene therapy trial at the University of Pennsylvania, doctors injected Gelsinger's liver with a cold virus that had been modified to carry a gene to correct OTC.[4]

After Gelsinger received the treatment, he developed a high fever and fell into a coma. His organs then failed and he died. Gelsinger's father, who gave permission for his son to participate in the study, said he thought the procedure would cause only a mild reaction in his son. He said no one told him that a monkey had died in a similar experiment or that another patient had suffered serious side effects.[5]

After Jesse Gelsinger's death, a United States

Senate subcommittee held hearings. In February 2000, committee members determined that there were problems with many gene therapy programs. Too many researchers were not complying with the National Institutes of Health requirements to report harmful effects of experiments. The investigation into the circumstances of Gelsinger's death would continue, but in the meantime the U.S. Food and Drug Administration stopped human gene therapy experiments at the University of Pennsylvania.[6]

The Common Rule

One concern that arose from Jesse Gelsinger's death was that some gene therapy researchers were not telling participants of potential risks and benefits. After the end of World War II, horror stories emerged about how Nazi scientists conducted medical experiments on prisoners. To prevent this from happening again, most industrialized countries passed rules to protect human subjects in future clinical experiments. In the United States, this code of conduct was called the Common Rule.

The Common Rule, as revised by the federal government in 1981, requires researchers to fully inform all persons who agree to take part in clinical trials. If a minor (person under the legal age of consent) is taking part in a clinical trial, then that person's legal guardian must be thoroughly informed. The process is called informed consent. Research subjects must know all the possible risks, as well as benefits, of any experiment. If experiments are in early stages and no benefit can soon be expected, volunteers must be told. In such a case, subjects may agree to take part simply to help further research.

The National Research Act of 1974 gave legal protection to volunteers who take part in medical research funded by the federal government. The act provided for institutional review boards (IRBs) that would oversee human research to be sure that experiments are scientifically and ethically sound. In 1999, however, the federal government determined that many IRBs were too underfunded and overburdened to monitor human clinical trials as they should. As a result, the government stopped all human research at several institutions, including Duke University Medical Center, Rush-Presbyterian-St. Luke's Medical Center in Chicago, and West Los Angeles Medical Center.[7]

Federal rules are in force only when a research facility receives federal funds. Since most modern gene therapy research is privately funded, much of the work does not come under government supervision. Besides lack of government supervision, private funding also means that research information may not always be shared. Researchers working in federally funded programs are required to share information. However, when a company funds gene therapy research, profits are at stake, and scientists are often asked to keep information about the project secret. This hoarding of information can keep patients and the general public from learning of any harmful effects of gene therapy experiments.[8]

Genetically Engineered Drugs and Hormones

Gene therapy is one method being explored for the treatment of inherited diseases. A second way that genes can be used to treat diseases is through bio-engineered drugs. Bioengineered drugs are made by plants or animals that have been genetically altered to produce the drug. Some bioengineered drugs may be given to a patient to change the function of one or more genes in the body. Bioengineered products used in this way include human insulin; human growth hormone (HGH); bovine growth hormone (BGH), a

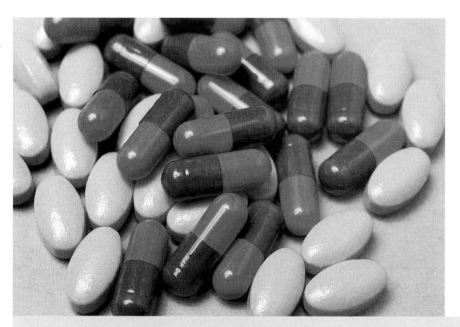

One exciting benefit of gene research is gene therapy—the use of medication to treat inherited diseases.

substance given to cattle to increase milk production; and Factor VIII, a drug given to patients with hemophilia.

The medicines listed above are made by genetically engineering a bacteria to produce the substance. In insulin production, for example, the gene for human insulin is inserted into a bacteria's DNA, which causes the bacteria to produce the hormone. Similar technology is used in the production of human growth hormone, bovine growth hormone, and Factor VIII. Human growth hormone may be given to children who have inherited the gene for dwarfism. Injected at regular intervals throughout childhood, the drug helps these children grow to normal height. Bovine growth hormone is given to cows to increase milk production. Factor VIII helps hemophilia patients' blood clot.

Experiments are under way to genetically engineer sheep, cows, pigs, and other animals to produce hormones and other substances medically advantageous to humans. By inserting the genes for Factor VIII in cows, for example, scientists hope to create cattle whose milk produces the substance. The substance could be extracted from the bioengineered cows' milk and given to persons whose blood lacks the clotting factor.

Methods Used in Gene Therapy

Scientists are hopeful that gene therapy, if we can perfect it, can become a useful weapon against some terrible inherited diseases and malformations. At present, gene therapy is still in the early stages of development, and, as is typical of any therapy, it does not always work as planned. Scientists can put new DNA into cells they want to improve, but inserting the DNA so it reaches the right destination is a major problem. Sometimes diseased or dysfunctional cells are removed from the patient, and healthy DNA is injected into them. The "corrected" cells are grown in large numbers, then injected back into the patient. Another method of getting new DNA into a patient's cells is to use a carrier. Carriers are usually viruses that have been rendered harmless. The virus cells are injected with the DNA intended to help the patient. The viruses are also given the capacity to recognize target cells. When the modified virus cells are injected into the patient, ideally they will enter the right cells and deliver the DNA they carry.

Currently neither of the above methods works all the time. Injecting a patient with his or her own DNA-modified cells usually ensures that some of the desired DNA is delivered. But doctors do not yet know how many cells are needed to do the job. And withdrawing too many cells from a patient can be harmful.

When viruses are used as DNA carriers, for one reason or another they often do not reach the cells that need the new DNA. For gene therapy to be reliable, the replacement DNA must not only reach targeted cells, it must find its way into the right place on the chromosomes. If the new DNA reaches a spot in between genes on a chromosome, it could sit there doing nothing for the patient. So far, scientists have found ways to insert a DNA control system to activate the new genes once they are inserted, but the system is still hit and miss. Too often gene therapy fails because either the new genes do not reach their destinations or they do not perform once they get to the patient's cells. In some forms of severe combined immune deficiency, gene therapy has been successful because the inserted gene that produces a protein critical to the immune system is constantly switched on. When the protein is produced even in small amounts, the patients show marked improvement.[9]

Gene therapy is still in its infancy, but scientists hope to see regular, positive results within the next five to ten years. The argument will continue for some time, however, over whether or not we should change a person's genetic makeup.

4

Genetic Testing

In 1991, Jeff Pinard was a freshman majoring in microbiology at the University of Michigan. He had chosen the school and his major mostly because of a disease he had grown up with called cystic fibrosis (CF). The disease, which causes a thick mucus to be deposited in the lungs, is inherited. For the disease to show up in an individual, he or she has to have inherited both recessive genes for the disease—one from each parent. More than 10 million Americans of northern European descent, or one in thirty-one individuals in the United States, carry a recessive gene for CF. Carriers have no symptoms, but they can pass the gene on to their children. When two carriers conceive a child, there is a 25 percent chance that the child will have CF. About thirty thousand children and adults in the United States have cystic fibrosis.[1]

Pinard wanted to help with the University of Michigan's research in CF, so he volunteered to work in the lab. He proved so adept at the work that the Cystic Fibrosis Foundation gave him a grant, and twenty-year-old Pinard spent the summer after his sophomore year working forty to fifty hours a week on the project. He and the other CF researchers at the university worked to locate all of the mutations on genes responsible for the disease. Pinard's research was helped by the fact that tests already exist for finding the most common gene for CF in individuals who are carriers. But the University of Michigan scientists hoped their work would lead to more effective treatments for the disease, or maybe even a cure.

Pinard's interest in CF research was personal. All of his life he had been hospitalized several times a year with bacterial infections in his lungs. The infections were treated with antibiotics that could damage his liver. Just to keep breathing, Pinard had to be pounded on the chest and back in eleven different positions for at least an hour every day to loosen the mucus in his lungs. The thick CF mucus also clogs the pancreas. This prevents enzymes from reaching the intestines to help break down food. So Pinard also took five pancreatic enzyme pills at mealtimes, just so he could digest his food. He knew that most

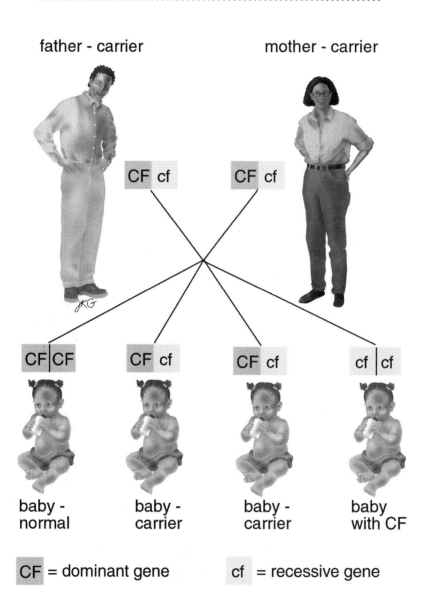

father - carrier   mother - carrier

CF cf   CF cf

CF CF   CF cf   CF cf   cf cf

baby -   baby -   baby -   baby
normal   carrier   carrier   with CF

CF = dominant gene   cf = recessive gene

Cystic fibrosis is inherited. A screening test has now been developed to locate the most common gene that carries the disease.

CF patients die before age thirty, usually from lung problems that lead to heart failure, or from liver damage.

As a student scientist, Pinard tested his own DNA and that of others, searching for CF gene mutations. Francis Collins, who was Pinard's supervisor and later became director of the National Human Genome Research Institute, said of the young researcher, "He was all enthusiasm, good humor, smarts . . ." and he "had a fairly profound effect on my lab."[2] Pinard's work was cut short when his illness forced him to drop out of school. In December 1999, he was living at home and working as a computer consultant for a utilities company.[3]

Genetic Tests Become More Available

Thanks to Jeff Pinard and other researchers, cystic fibrosis is just one of the genetic diseases for which screening tests have been developed. Some forty different genes are associated with CF, but a test has been developed for the most common one, which is found in about 75 percent of cystic fibrosis patients.[4] There are an estimated four thousand known genetic diseases, but tests do not yet exist to detect genes for all of them. Currently, some 4 million genetic tests are performed each year in the United States.[5] In addition to cystic fibrosis, tests exist to detect the genes responsible for diseases such as the following:

- hemochromatosis, the most common genetic disease in the United States

- some forms of breast, ovarian, and colon cancer

- spinocerebellar ataxia, a rare disorder that gradually destroys the brain's cerebellum

- Huntington's disease

- Down syndrome, a disease that causes mental retardation and other problems

- fragile X disease

- Tay-Sachs, a disease that affects some people of Jewish descent

- Gaucher's disease, which affects fat metabolism

- sickle-cell anemia, a disorder of the red blood cells most often diagnosed in African Americans

Newborn babies are routinely checked for sickle-cell anemia, inherited thyroid disease, and phenylketonuria (PKU).[6]

The genetic basis for diseases that arise from just one gene, such as sickle-cell anemia and Huntington's disease, are easiest for scientists to determine. Since they follow predictable genetic patterns when they are passed from parents to children, they can be tracked through families. Tracking the genetic roots of more complex disorders, such as cystic fibrosis, multiple sclerosis, heart disease, and cancer, is more difficult. This is because the disorders are caused by several genes working together and because the disorders are affected by other factors, such as the environment and personal health habits.

Does It Run in My Family?

As in Jeff Pinard's research, tests for genes that cause disease can give important information to researchers. Such tests are also helpful to individuals who are concerned that a genetic disease runs in the family. Once testing reveals the genes, the DNA from volunteers can be used to research treatments and cures. Testing for some diseases is also available to people who want to find out if they carry the gene for a particular affliction. Those individuals who choose to take a genetic test for reasons other than scientific research usually:

- have a family history of a specific disease

- may show symptoms of a genetic disorder

- are concerned about passing on a genetic disorder to offspring

Deciding whether or not to have a genetic test can be hard because some diseases, such as Huntington's and fragile X disease, have no cure or effective treatment. Some people want to learn whether or not they carry the gene for hemochromatosis, Huntington's disease, fragile X, or other inherited disorders so they can plan their lives accordingly. Others would perhaps be so upset to learn that they have such a gene that they could not enjoy their lives at all. For this reason, anyone thinking about genetic testing should consider what effect the results will have on his or her life.

Hemochromatosis causes the body to store too much iron in the blood. Treatment consists of periodically drawing off blood. If left untreated, a patient's joints ache, his or her hair falls out, and he or she is tired all the time. Untreated sufferers can eventually die of organ failure.

Huntington's disease is a disease of the central nervous system which is caused by the inheritance of a dominant gene. About one in every ten thousand people is affected. If one parent has Huntington's disease and carries the normal gene (Hh),and the other parent does not have the disease (hh), each child has

Renowned folk singer Woody Guthrie suffered from Huntington's disease, a genetic illness. His son, folk singer Arlo Guthrie, also inherited the disease.

a 50 percent chance of inheriting the disease. If the parent with Huntington's has two dominant genes for the disease (HH), each child will develop the disease. (Since the gene is dominant, if it is passed from parent to offspring, the disease will develop.) Huntington's disease usually shows up between the ages of thirty and fifty. The patient becomes irrational and sometimes violent. Slurred speech and irregular body movements are also typical. There is no cure for the disease, which is eventually fatal.

Before a genetic test was developed for Huntington's, family members with relatives who died of the disease simply had to wait until they reached middle age to see if they, too, would become ill. By this time many had already had children, passing on the gene for Huntington's. Now, if a person finds out through genetic testing that he or she carries the gene for Huntington's disease, that person can make the difficult decision not to have children. There is presently no preventive measure to keep carriers from developing the disease.

Fragile X is the most common inherited cause of mental retardation. It is identified by a break, or weakness, on the long arm of the X chromosome. Since it is a mutation of a sex chromosome, like hemophilia, it is called a sex-linked disorder. The gene is not clearly dominant or recessive. The degree of mental retardation and other symptoms present in those who inherit the disease depends upon the extent of the mutation of the X chromosome. Since the condition is inherited only through the X chromosome, mothers are carriers and their sons are at risk of being affected. Daughters are at risk of being carriers and sometimes are affected, but usually more mildly than sons. Fragile X cannot be transmitted from father to son, because the Y chromosome is not involved. Twenty percent of people who have the fragile X gene will never show any signs of mental retardation.

Inheriting a gene associated with a disorder does not mean that the disorder will develop. The likelihood of developing the disease can be 100 percent, as in the case of the gene for Huntington's, or it can be very low. Some people who inherit a gene or genes for a disorder may develop mild forms of the disease that require no treatment, while in others the disease may quickly progress and resist all forms of treatment. Multiple sclerosis is an example of an inherited disorder that may be mild or rapidly progressing and disabling.

Genetic tests for such complex disorders as breast cancer and heart disease may indicate whether or not there is a genetic basis for these diseases. Again, however, just because people carry a gene or genes for an inherited disease does not mean they will get the disease. Many environmental factors such as the following also affect the onset of some genetic diseases:

- geographic location
- general nutritional state
- personal health habits
- socioeconomic level

- access to health care

- exposure to pollutants and chemicals, including alcohol and recreational drugs

The Testing Process

Genetic testing is a complex process. Blood is drawn, cells are swabbed from the inside of the cheek, or samples of other body tissues and fluids may be taken. The DNA is extracted, then techniques are used to examine the genes directly.

When the gene for a disease cannot be located, indirect testing may be used. This involves using DNA from other family members to see if similar patterns occur.

Special training is required to perform DNA tests and a specialist should analyze the results. Once testing is completed, individuals who are tested should receive genetic counseling to help them make decisions based on the information they have received. Genetic counseling is a relatively new specialty in the mental health field. Counselors who are well versed in the symptoms of genetic diseases and the way they are inherited can help families make sense of DNA test results and plan for the future.

Who Should Be Tested?

By 1999, genetic screening for cystic fibrosis could identify 90 percent of carriers. This meant that, when carriers were married, the test could detect 81 percent of the couples at risk for having a child with cystic fibrosis. This also gave rise to many questions.

Who should be tested? Should everyone be tested, including those groups who are unlikely to have CF genes? (The incidence of CF in African Americans is just one-tenth that of whites, and Asians almost never get the disease.) At what age should people be tested? A national panel of scientists offered these recommendations in 1997:

- All pregnant women and their husbands should be offered the option to be tested for CF genes.

- People with family histories of CF and their mates should be offered the testing option.

- Insurance should cover the cost of the tests.[7]

Generally, people may opt for genetic testing at different stages in their lives. Couples whose families have a history of recessive genetic disorders may want to be tested to see if either individual is a carrier for the disorder, as part of planning to have a baby. If both members of the couple are carriers for a specific disorder, sometimes the couple decides not to have children, or they may decide to accept the risk of having a child with that disorder.

Genetic testing of a baby before it is born is also possible when there is a risk that the developing child will have a genetic disorder. A few defects can now be corrected with microsurgery while the baby is still in the womb. However, abortion may be presented as an option when the genetic disorder is considered severe. There is much controversy over whether or not unborn children should be aborted when tests are positive for a severe genetic disorder.

Genetic testing is also available to couples using reproductive technology, such as in vitro fertilization (IVF), to conceive. IVF involves harvesting eggs from women, fertilizing them in the laboratory, then implanting the resulting embryos into the mother's womb. Genetic screening at the embryo stage allows parents using IVF to have embryos tested before they are implanted in the womb. Genetic screening begins at the eight-cell stage of embryo development. At this time, a cell is removed from the embryo in the laboratory and allowed to duplicate. These cells are then screened for a specific genetic disorder. If none is found, the embryo can then be implanted into the mother's womb and carried to term. Defective embryos are destroyed. This, too, is a controversial procedure, since many may consider destruction of defective embryos abortion.

The first live birth after pre-implantation genetic screening occurred in London in 1992. The parents were both cystic fibrosis carriers. They had used IVF and had the resultant embryos screened for CF before choosing one for implantation that did not have the genes for CF. The result was a healthy baby girl named Chloe.[8]

A fourth type of genetic testing involves identifying a DNA sample as belonging to a specific individual. This is possible because, except for identical twins, no two people have the same DNA "fingerprint." To determine the true parents of a child, for example, one or both parents may be tested to see if their DNA is similar to that of the child. DNA testing may also be used to identify accident or crime victims or even casualties in war time. Law enforcement agencies may also use DNA testing to link an individual to a specific crime or to rule out a person as a suspect. Many people allege that the tests are not foolproof, but some individuals arrested for crimes in the United States and other countries now have their DNA profiles on file for future reference.

DNA Tests Used to Prove Guilt and Innocence

DNA tests have proved especially valuable in law enforcement. In 1987, Robert Melias, a resident of Great Britain, was the first person convicted of a crime (rape) on the basis of DNA evidence. In November 1987, in Orange County, Florida, Tommy Lee Andrews became one of the first persons in the United States to be convicted of the crime of rape based on DNA evidence.[9]

As DNA tests have become more reliable, DNA evidence has also been used to free criminals who were found guilty at trial and jailed. For example, in July 1999, Vincent Jenkins was freed from the Green Haven Correctional Facility in New York. He had served nearly seventeen years of a life sentence for a rape he did not commit. DNA tests were not available when Jenkins was first arrested, but they were later used to rule out Jenkins as the man who attacked a woman in Buffalo in 1982.[10]

In 1992, attorneys Barry Scheck and Peter Neufeld started the Innocence Project at the Benjamin N. Cardozo School of Law in Manhattan,

New York, to help investigate cases like Jenkins. In 1999, the convictions of sixty-four people in the United States had been overturned as a result of DNA testing. The inmates were then released from prison. In eight of the cases, the prison inmates were on death row.[11] The Innocence Project helped in over thirty-six of the sixty-four cases. In May 2000, the Innocence Project was handling more than two hundred cases in which DNA testing could be a factor in overturning a conviction.[12]

Other Uses for DNA Tests

DNA tests are also proving useful in other ways. For instance, in May 2000, researchers at the University of Pittsburgh reported that doctors would soon be able to use genetic tests to tell which transplant patients are most likely to reject a donated organ. Two groups of patients were tested: those who had rejected transplanted organs and those who had not. Those patients who had not rejected donor organs had genes that triggered secretions of higher levels of substances in the blood that help strengthen the immune system. One goal of the study was to help transplant patients stop taking anti-rejection drugs. Those patients who tested unlikely to reject a donor organ could most likely stop taking the drugs.[13]

In June 2000, Wyoming became the first state to sponsor a DNA testing project for parents and children called Project LifePrint. Volunteers from the Wyoming Cops Association took DNA samples from children by using cheek swabs and then sealed the samples in sterilized kits. Parents were instructed to keep the samples at home and give them to law enforcement authorities for analysis if their children were ever missing. The samples would be used to identify children in these situations.[14]

Ethical, Legal, and Social Issues in Genetic Testing

Because information from genetic testing can greatly affect the lives of those tested, careful handling of this information is important. It is essential that knowledge gained from testing not be abusive. The rights of those tested must be protected. To do so, several issues must be considered. The most serious of those issues include:

Privacy and confidentiality. Tested individuals have the right to privacy. If a person is found to carry a gene that makes him or her or future offspring likely to develop a genetic disorder and this information is released, that person's ability to get a job or to buy insurance might be affected.

Since genetic information is sensitive, access should be limited to those authorized to receive results, such as physicians. Future access to genetic testing results should also be limited, because of the possibility of genetic discrimination.

Informed consent. Physicians must get permission, in writing, from the person to be tested, or from his or her legal guardian. Anyone seeking genetic testing must be thoroughly informed about the risks, benefits, effectiveness, and alternatives to testing before tests are performed.

As new tests are developed, care should be taken to see that results are accurate. And those who are tested should always receive counseling before proceeding on any course that could change their lives.

5

Genetic Discrimination, Privacy, and Civil Liberties

Jamie Stephenson's health insurance company found out that her son had a genetic disorder that causes mental retardation. The company canceled her family's health insurance.[1]

Theresa Morelli was a young, single attorney who applied for a disability insurance policy. The policy would provide funds in case she was ever injured and could not work. The insurance company obtained Morelli's medical records and discovered her father had Huntington's disease. The company told Morelli she would have to wait until she was fifty, to see if she developed symptoms for

71

Huntington's disease. If she did not show symptoms of the disease by that time, they would give her a policy.[2]

In December 1999, Terri Seargent, a forty-three-year-old office manager, was fired after she tested positive for the genetic disease from which her brother died. Seargent had begun receiving treatments for the disease. She was fired when her self-insured employer got the first medical bill.[3]

The first two cases listed above were among more than two hundred examples of genetic discrimination reported by Stanford University and Harvard Medical School researchers in April 1996.[4] The third case was reported in the April 10, 2000, issue of *Newsweek* magazine.[5] Genetic discrimination means that individuals are treated differently based on their genetic makeup or family history, even if they show no symptoms of a disorder. Discrimination is most likely to occur when people are applying for jobs or for insurance. But it has also been documented in schools, the military, and when couples apply to adopt children.

Concern about the abuse of genetic information is increasing because of the growing number of tests for inherited diseases. Soon after a new genetic disease is found, biotechnology companies develop a diagnostic test for it. "But every time we invent a new genetic test, we can get more information about you," Boston University bioethicist George Annas told *USA Today*.[6] More information is also available because we now know more about how genes can be passed down in families.

Most experts agree that genetic discrimination will grow, unless laws are in place to prevent it. Thirty-nine states have laws prohibiting discrimination in health insurance based on genetic tests. Fifteen states have passed legislation forbidding genetic discrimination in employment.[7] In 1997, Congress passed the Health Insurance Portability and Accountability Act (HIPAA). The act prevents health insurers from denying coverage based on genetic information. However, it applies only to people moving between group plans. In February 2000, President Bill Clinton signed an Executive Order banning the federal government from using genetic data in employment decisions.

Under the order, the government cannot request or require job applicants or employees to take genetic tests. And the government cannot use information from such tests in hiring or promotion decisions.

"Today, powerful ways of technological change threaten to erode our sacred walls of privacy in ways we could not have envisioned a generation ago," Clinton said in a speech introducing the order. "Americans are genuinely worried genetic information will be used against them."[8]

The Americans With Disabilities Act (ADA) of 1990 also offers some protection against genetic discrimination in the workplace. It protects against discrimination those who have a genetic condition or disease, or are regarded as having a disability. Under a 1995 ruling by the Equal Employment Opportunities Commission, the ADA applies to anyone who is discriminated against on the basis of genetic

President Clinton proposed legislation that would bar health insurance companies from discriminating against apparently healthy people on the basis of their genetic background. In this photo, he is talking to Mary Jo Kahn, whose family has a history of cancer.

information relating to illness, disease, condition, or other disorders. The ADA does not cover insurance companies.[9]

The Harvard-Stanford study mentioned in the chapter introduction was conducted by Lisa N. Geller, of the Department of Neurobiology and Division of Medical Ethics at Harvard Medical School. She and her colleagues found that genetic discrimination was more widespread in the United States than people thought. Geller questioned volunteers who carried genes that could cause a disease, but who had not yet developed symptoms. People used in the survey had genes for Huntington's disease, mucopolysaccaridosis (MPS), phenylketonuria (PKU), and hemochromatosis. MPS can cause mental retardation. PKU also causes mental retardation, but is nearly always discovered in infancy and can be prevented with a special diet.

Of the 917 responses received by Geller and her associates, 455 (about half) reported some form of genetic discrimination. Genetic discrimination was reported in health and life insurance companies, health care providers, blood banks, adoption agencies, the military, and schools.[10]

Discrimination in Insurance, Adoption, Employment, and Schools

One of the most common forms of genetic discrimination reported in surveys is denial of health insurance based on a person's genetic test results. Access to medical records often means that genetic information is revealed to insurance companies, which then deny insurance coverage.

As reported in Geller's study:

- A health maintenance organization (HMO) had paid health expenses for a child since birth. After the child was diagnosed with MPS, the HMO refused to pay for physical therapy, even though the therapy had been previously approved. The HMO said it did not have to pay because the child's condition was present before the family enrolled in the HMO. The family complained to a customer service representative of the HMO and payment was made.

- A health insurance company in Colorado canceled a couple's insurance when their three-year-old child was diagnosed with MPS. The couple threatened to sue the company and the policy was reinstated. However, the new policy contained a rider that denied coverage for two common MPS complications.[11]

According to Geller, genetic testing has also been reported as the source for discrimination in adoption. One couple was turned down for adoption because the mother was at risk for developing Huntington's disease. A biological mother with Huntington's disease was not allowed to place her baby for adoption with a state adoption agency.

In another case, because the wife was at risk for Huntington's disease, a couple was told they could only adopt a child who was also at risk for Huntington's disease.[12]

Employers often purchase group health insurance

plans for their employees. Therefore, they have a financial interest in hiring those workers whom they believe are most likely to stay healthy. This practice puts at risk of genetic discrimination those employees who have the genetic makeup to develop a genetic disorder. For example, Geller reported that a social worker who had earned several promotions and high performance evaluations was dismissed from her job when it was learned that she could develop Huntington's disease.[13]

In another incident, a healthy young man who carried one recessive gene for Gaucher's disease was not allowed to enlist in the military, even though one gene for the condition does not cause the disease.[14] Gaucher's disease affects fat metabolism. It can cause an enlarged spleen, abnormal skin pigmentation, and bone lesions.

In other cases of genetic discrimination, African Americans who carried the recessive gene for sickle-cell anemia were denied admission to the U.S. Air Force Academy. Grounds for denial were based on the assumption that they might not be able to stand the reduced-oxygen environment present in high-altitude flights. This was untrue. People with sickle-cell anemia have sickle-shaped, instead of round, red blood cells, but a person must have two genes for the disorder before it appears. A person with one gene for sickle-cell anemia does not develop the disease.[15]

In the 1970s, the United States carried out a screening program for sickle-cell anemia, which affects one in four hundred African Americans. There were few genetic counselors at that time, and the

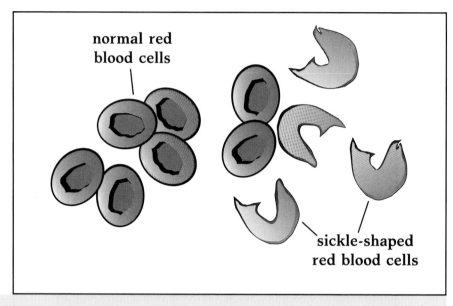

normal red
blood cells

sickle-shaped
red blood cells

Genetic discrimination is a real and present danger. At one time, African Americans who carried the recessive gene for sickle-cell anemia were denied admission to the U.S. Air Force Academy. But a person with one recessive gene does not develop the disease.

screening program was not properly introduced or explained. As a result, many of those who learned they were carriers of the recessive sickle-cell gene mistakenly thought they had the disease. Some husbands and wives who were carriers were told that they should avoid having children. That advice led to charges of racism.[16]

In *Exploding the Gene Myth*, Ruth Hubbard and Elijah Wald warn schools against using genetic testing to predict or explain those children who have learning disabilities. Learning disabilities are most often not caused by a child's genes.[17]

Geller's study also found a few incidents of genetic discrimination in schools. In one small school district, for example, two healthy children attended the same school as their disabled brother. The brother had MPS and was enrolled in special education. When one of the healthy children, who was in second grade, showed poor penmanship skills, the teacher decided this child might also have MPS. Without consulting the child's parents or a doctor, the teacher sent the child back to first grade. The parents protested and the child was returned to second grade.[18]

Privacy Issues

Genetic test results usually become part of a person's medical record. Since genetic test results can lead to genetic discrimination, those results must be kept private. If people are found to be carriers or likely to develop an inherited disease, these findings, if released, could affect the future employability or insurability of those individuals. Legally, patients must give their consent, in writing, for their medical records to be released to a third party.

Medical records are kept in many locations, such as hospitals, clinics, and doctors' offices. They are also kept in central locations such as the Medical Information Bureau. Genetic test results are entered in a person's medical records, and insurance companies have access to those records. Insurance companies use medical information to predict a person's risk of illness and death. They use such risk information to decide which individuals and groups they will insure and at what price. If insurance is denied, a person may not be able to pay for health care. Therefore, the information in medical records helps determine who has access to health care.

It is also important that people give their informed consent, in writing, for genetic testing. Before any person is tested, he or she should know the risks, benefits, effectiveness, and alternatives. After testing, individuals should be counseled by a professional who can explain test results and help them make decisions based on those results. Some bioethicists say that it is unethical to test children for a genetic disease that has no cure. Parents should wait until their children are legally of age and better able to face discouraging results.

Ethical and Social Issues

Genetic testing can deeply affect lives. Not only can the results force hard decisions, but the potential for misuse and abuse is also a concern. For instance, many fear that the motivation for testing may go beyond looking for genetic disorders, and the scope of testing may someday be used to create the "perfect" child. What if parents want to raise a son (or daughter), and the developing baby is not of the desired sex? What if the child is found to have genes that could cause learning disorders, but may or may not be expressed as the child grows? How far should humans go in "improving" their genetic makeup?

The idea that genetic testing may allow humans

to produce superior children and thus improve the species is the concept called eugenics. In the early 1900s, many well-known Americans accepted eugenics as the answer to reducing crime, poverty, and other social ills. Proponents of the eugenics movement claimed that these conditions exist because certain classes of people had "inferior" genes. The American eugenics movement began in 1904, with genetics professor Charles Davenport of the University of Chicago as its director. Well-known Americans who endorsed eugenics policies included United States presidents Theodore Roosevelt and Calvin Coolidge; horticulturist Luther Burbank; David Starr Jordan, president of Stanford University; Francis Galton, the cousin of Charles Darwin; Mrs. E. H. Harriman, wife of railroad and telegraph businessman E. H. Harriman; and J. H. Kellogg, founder of Kellogg foods. Davenport persuaded Mrs. Harriman to buy land at Cold Spring Harbor, New York, to establish a Eugenics Record Office, which would collect reports, articles, charts, and pedigrees to prove that certain "inferior" traits, such as shiftlessness, were inherited.[19]

Two historical events discredited the eugenics movement.

1. The Great Depression of the 1930s proved that no one race or type of people are immune to poverty, regardless of heredity.

2. Hitler's rise to power in Europe after 1933 soon ended America's fascination with eugenics.

As the technology for genetic engineering improves, many people fear that the idea that genetics

Proponents of eugenics believe that crime and other social issues exist because of people with "inferior" genes. Among those who endorsed such a theory was Calvin Coolidge, who became president of the United States in 1924.

alone can improve society's ills will again become popular. Again, education is the key. The more people learn about genetics and inherited traits, the less likely they will be to believe the untrue allegations that fueled the eugenics movement. In short, improved knowledge of genetics and enlightened government polices are most likely to prevent all forms of genetic discrimination.

6

The Gene Business

Imagine that you are a scientist, helping to develop a genetically engineered drug that could target one or more of the genes responsible for aging. By taking this miracle pill, every adult could delay, maybe for a long time, wrinkled, thinning skin and hair loss. The magic pill might even prevent osteoporosis (a bone thinning disease), arthritis (a painful condition of the joints), cancer, clogged arteries, and heart disease. Imagine, too, that you are a shareholder in the drug company that is paying for your research. You will become rich beyond your wildest dreams because surely every adult in the world will want to take this

84

drug. Despite your desire to help others, would you be tempted to rush the product to market, ignoring some side effects of the drug that do not seem too harmful?

Now imagine a slightly different situation. Say the drug was developed by medical researchers who used blood taken from hospital patients in their research. While you were in the hospital, researchers tested a sample of your blood and discovered it had large quantities of a protein that boosts immunity. Without telling you, the researchers used your blood samples for an important new study. A university paid for the research and patented the material taken from your cells. You did not know about the project. When an expensive drug was developed, you did not share in the profits. You find out that your blood was used, and now you wonder if, as a donor, you should have been told that your blood could lead to the development of a valuable product. You also ask yourself how anyone else could own tissue that came from your body. Aren't you the sole owner of your own body tissue, and therefore entitled to a share of the drug company's profits?

Situations much like those above are now reality as genetics research has become a moneymaking business. Biotechnology companies invest huge sums of money to develop drugs and other products. Therefore, they claim, it is important to determine ownership at all stages of research. Ownership of new products is important, but questions of ethics are just as important. Unfortunately, ethics are frequently pushed aside in favor of profits.

The following questions about ethics and the business of genetics are often asked:

- Should those researchers involved in developing a genetically engineered plant, animal, or substance also have a direct financial stake in its potential profits?

- If scientists are associated economically with biotech or drug companies, can they objectively report research results?

- Will scientists with a monetary stake in a genetically engineered product truthfully inform subjects or the public about possible risks and side effects?

When scientists have a financial stake in their research, the most obvious danger is that they will make decisions based on profit and loss, rather than patient safety. Another danger is that companies that hire researchers often pressure them to keep silent about work in progress and to withhold data. "Today, most senior biologists are entangled with one or many companies," said David Baltimore, Nobel Prize winner and president of the California Institute of Technology, in February 2000. "Does it make people so biased they cannot think properly? I am (on) the board of (biotech company) Amgen, and I would have to think twice before arguing that drug prices are unconscionably high."[1]

It is still unclear how or if the questions listed above will be resolved. Some scientists agree with Alan Schechter of the National Institutes of Health (NIH), who says that any scientist who stands to make money from a study should not be allowed to do the research. Those scientists should voluntarily withdraw themselves from studies-for-profit.[2]

Many scientists also agree with Maynard V. Olson, professor of genetics at the University of Washington in Seattle, who says that a traditional sharing of information among scientists is most ethical. Scientists, he says, should review published studies in journals, then build on each other's work.[3]

Ethical Guidelines for Scientists

The American Medical Association's (AMA's) *Code of Medical Ethics* lists guidelines in many areas, for any member physician engaged in genetics counseling or research. In all situations, the AMA guidelines stress that doctors must put the patient before research goals or profit. They also emphasize the importance of doctors getting informed consent from any person who becomes a research subject. Participants must know any benefits or risks associated with the procedure.

The National Institutes of Health in Bethesda, Maryland, also has a detailed code of ethics for scientific and medical researchers. Abiding by existing rules is a must for researchers, says Lana Skirboll, director of the NIH Office of Scientific Policy. In a February 2000 article for *USA Today*, Skirboll said more guidelines probably are not needed, but "there will be legislation unless scientists have open discussions about conflict of interest," and follow existing guidelines for ethical conduct.[4]

Code of Ethics

I. Physicians shall provide competent medical service with compassion and respect for human dignity.

II. Physicians shall deal honestly with patients and colleagues, and work to expose those physicians who are incompetent, or who engage in fraud or deception.

III. Physicians shall respect the law and also work to change any requirements that are against the best interests of the patient.

IV. Physicians shall respect the rights of patients, colleagues, and other health professionals. They shall keep patient confidences as required by law.

V. Physicians shall work to study, apply, and advance scientific knowledge. They shall also inform patients, colleagues, and the public, and consult other health care professionals when appropriate.

VI. Physicians shall, except in emergencies, be free to choose patients, associates, and the environment in which they provide medical services.

VII. Whenever possible, physicians shall work to improve the community.

The American Medical Association's Code of Ethics *lists guidelines for any member physician engaged in genetics counseling or research.*

Some Landmark Legal Cases

One of the first cases of conflict of interest in a biotechnology matter was published in the early 1990s in *Genewatch* by the Council for Responsible Genetics located in Cambridge, Massachusetts. Dr. Scheffer Tseng, a researcher at the Harvard-affiliated Massachusetts Eye and Ear Infirmary, tested a vitamin A ointment to cure "dry-eye syndrome," a severe eye problem. While he was a research fellow at Harvard, Dr. Tseng was also a paid consultant of and a principal shareholder in Spectra Pharmaceutical Inc. Spectra produced the drug Dr. Tseng was testing.

It was determined that Dr. Tseng used the experimental drug on five times more patients than were approved in his research plan. He allegedly also tested the drug on patients without their consent. He was also said to have exaggerated the benefits of the drug.

Dr. Tseng's claims of success for the drug were backed by his Harvard supervisor, Kenneth Kenyon, and by Edward Maumenee, Spectra's founder. Charges filed with the Massachusetts medical board against Dr. Tseng and Kenneth Kenyon were later dismissed.[5] The case may be an extreme example of conflict of interest. But it illustrates how research results may be less than reliable when researchers have a financial stake in the end product.

The second example presented at the beginning of this chapter is also based on a true event. In 1984, John Moore, an Alaskan businessman, was treated at the University of California at Los Angeles (UCLA) for a rare cancer. During his treatment, a doctor and researcher made a promising discovery. He discovered that tissue from Moore's spleen produced a blood protein that encourages the growth of cancer-fighting white blood cells.

Without Moore's knowledge or consent, university scientists created a cell line from Moore's tissue. They obtained a patent on their invention, which was worth about $3 billion in potential profits. Somehow

illegal growth-enhancing substances for years. He took steroids and human growth hormone. He said he believed when he took the drugs that they would give him the power and strength he needed to become a professional athlete. Alzado's doctor said the drugs probably also gave the athlete a rare form of brain cancer, of which he died in May 1992.[8]

Doctors often prescribe hGH injections for short children. Parents who want their short children to have the advantage they think height provides sometimes ask doctors for the drug, or the children themselves ask to take the drug. Many physicians oblige.

Then aging baby boomers discovered the drug, and demand again increased. According to Alan Mintz, M.D., sixty-two, founder of Cenegenics, a Las Vegas-based antiaging center, hGH does not simply slow the aging process, it actually reverses it. "I have only 8 percent body fat," he told *Modern Maturity* magazine. "I even have fewer wrinkles."[9]

But has hGH lived up to its hype? Not entirely. There are two important concerns. One is that the marketing campaign created to sell the drug created a "disease" or "abnormality" where none exists. Dr. John D. Lantos, of the Center for Clinical Medical Ethics at the University of Chicago, told *The New York Times* magazine that normal shortness was not a disease, until growth hormone became available. Once there was a "cure" for shortness (hGH), doctors prescribed it and insurance companies paid for it, and shortness was no longer seen as "healthy."[10]

The *New York Times* magazine article also

reported that hGH was given to boys with normal pituitary glands who were simply "too short" for their age. According to Genentech researchers quoted in the article, any child whose height falls within the lowest 3 percent of the population could be treated with hGH. By these standards, some ninety thousand children a year could receive the five-year drug treatment. This creates a possible market of some $9 billion per year for Genentech.[11]

A second concern about hGH is that the drug can be harmful. Unfortunately, many who take hGH have failed to consider the downside. Four reasons for people with normal pituitary glands to think again about treatment with hGH include:

1. The drug can cause serious side effects, including acromegaly (an overgrowth of bones of the hands, feet, and face), carpal tunnel syndrome, fluid buildup, joint and muscle pain, high blood pressure, and a higher risk of congestive heart failure. Some studies report more cases of leukemia in people treated with hGH. It may also stimulate tumor growth.[12]

2. The drug must be injected daily over a period of time, and long-term side effects are still unknown. The drug can actually slow normal growth when it is given to children with normal pituitary glands and they stop taking the drug.

3. A course of treatment with hGH is expensive, ranging from $8,000 to $15,000 per year, depending upon dosage. Costs are not usually covered by medical insurance.[13]

4. No proof exists that the treatment works. The journal *Physical Therapy* examined nine studies on hGH in 1999 and found increased muscle tissue in just four of the studies. A study published in *Annals of Internal Medicine* in 1996 found that healthy older male subjects showed an increase in muscle mass and reduced body fat, but no evidence of increased strength or physical performance. Some doctors claim that increases in body mass are due to water retention.[14]

Patenting Life

As biotechnology progresses, companies that fund research want to own results of their research, so that they can market the new products without fear of legal challenges. One way to guarantee ownership of new discoveries is to get a patent from the United States Patent and Trademark Office (PTO). A patent is the legal right to an invention or product. It grants its owner the exclusive right to license or sell the invention or product.

A patent for a genetically modified organism was first granted in 1980, after nearly ten years of court hearings. In 1970, Ananda Chakrabarty was an Indian microbiologist working for the General Electric Company. He applied to the United States Patents and Trademark Office for a patent on a microorganism that had been genetically altered to eat up oil spills in the oceans. The request was denied. The PTO claimed that existing patent law did not permit patenting living organisms.

Can living organisms be patented? That very question has been weighed in court. Other questions having to do with genetically altered plants, food, and people are likely to lead to future legal challenges.

The PTO's decision was appealed to the Court of Customs and Patent Appeals. In this court, Ananda Chakrabarty and General Electric won. The PTO appealed, and the case was eventually heard by the United States Supreme Court. The Supreme Court ruled in favor of Chakrabarty and granted the first patent on a genetically engineered organism. The Court held that Chakrabarty's organism was a "human-made invention," and therefore could be patented.

General Electric later decided not to sell the fragile organism because it could not survive in rough seas.[15] But the Court's decision opened the door for the patenting of genetically engineered organisms and materials. It also helped genetics research to become profitable.[16] The U.S. Patent and Trademark Office reinforced this position in 1987, when it held that any genetically engineered organism, whether plant or animal, can be patented.[17] Patents allow companies to make more money with their products because this means that others must pay a royalty fee to use a patented gene in any way.

Under current law, as scientists isolate genes responsible for certain diseases, such as sickle-cell anemia or some forms of cancer, they or their sponsors can patent the genes. This means that when a test is developed to see if a person has the gene, the individual or company who owns the patent can charge a fee. Many argue that high testing fees will mean that people with lower incomes cannot afford genetic tests that could benefit them.

A February 2000 review of a United States Patent and Trademark Office database by *USA Today* found that 30 of 171 federally funded scientists had been issued patents for gene therapy research. A scientist at the University of Pennsylvania who led the gene therapy study in which Jesse Gelsinger died held the largest number of patents.[18]

There is strong disagreement over whether patenting genes advances biotechnology or holds it back. Many biotechnology companies say they cannot spend huge sums for developing new drugs if other companies can copy it without paying royalty fees. But many public officials argue that patenting genes should not be allowed, because it discourages other researchers and adds unnecessary costs to new treatments. Some ethics experts claim that no one should be allowed to own genes or any form of living tissue. While the argument rages, companies that patent genes and genetic products collect royalty fees from testing laboratories and others. And consumers who take a genetic test or buy a bioengineered drug pay the price.

Human Bodies as Commodities?

As biotechnology became a growth industry, it raised the question: Is the human body also a product to be bought and sold? Advances in medical science, especially in the area of reproductive science, have created a demand for certain types of human tissue.

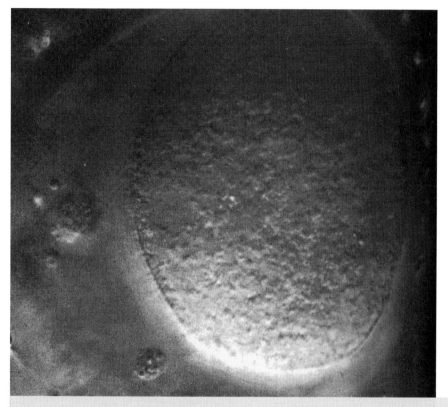

Everybody wants their children to have the greatest advantages. Why not start in the womb? Although human organs cannot be sold, no law says women cannot sell their eggs. One entrepreneur is selling the eggs of women considered beautiful on his Web site.

With the rise in genetic research, more and more ethical questions have surfaced. Arthur Caplan sits on a medical ethics panel at the University of Pennsylvania Medical Center. He has become a nationwide spokesman on medical ethics.

And when demand for a product is high, it usually follows that a high price will be set for that product. Federal law forbids the buying and selling of human organs for transplant, but other tissues may legally be sold, including blood, sperm, and eggs.

In 1999, Ron Harris, a commercial photographer, set up an Internet site to advertise for sale the eggs of several fashion models. "Choosing eggs from beautiful women will profoundly increase the success of your children and your children's children, for centuries to come," he advertised. Bidding was to start at $15,000, but it was unclear whether Harris had any takers. "It's a scam," Arthur Caplan, a bioethicist at the University of Pennsylvania, told *Newsweek* in November 1999. "A beautiful person will not necessarily beget a beautiful child."[19]

Harris's "eggs for sale" campaign disgusted many people. Shelley Smith, director of the Egg Donor Program in Los Angeles, said of Harris's scheme, "It's frightening and horrible, and the worst part for me is to think there might be something worse still beyond our imagination. It seems to escalate, and ever since the Internet it seems to snowball more rapidly, this depersonalization of people and selling of eggs."[20]

Smith's comments could also apply to the current profit-driven trend to market genetics research. An encouraging note, however, is that many scientists themselves see the need to follow conflict of interest guidelines in their research.

7

Genetics in Our Future

In May 2000, newspapers around the globe reported that every night, computers at sixteen biology laboratories around the world dialed up the National Institutes of Health in Bethesda, Maryland. The computers at NIH answered, then received strings of code that were put into a huge database. The letters in the code strings, representing the base pairs found in a DNA molecule, were always the same, but they were not always in the same order. Code strings looked something like this: ATAGCATCTCGGATC.[1]

Those letter strings are the language of the Human Genome Project, one of the most ambitious projects in the history of genetics research. Genome is the term for all of an organism's genetic information. Scientists around the world were part of the Human Genome Project, which was funded by the United States government. They set out to map the eighty thousand to one hundred thousand genes they believed existed within the twenty-three pairs of human chromosomes. The project was originally scheduled for completion in 2003, but it was finished ahead of time in mid-2000. The scientists were surprised to learn that instead of eighty thousand to one hundred thousand genes humans have just thirty thousand genes.[2] The scientists' work is readily available to other researchers, and it gave them a head start on learning how genes work, what they do, and why they sometimes do not work right.

In the United States, first the Department of Energy, and then the National Institutes of Health were the agencies responsible for organizing and carrying out the project. The project was begun in 1990 and was expected to take at least fifteen years to complete, but it progressed much faster than planned. Goals of the project were to:

- Locate each gene on all twenty-three pairs of human chromosomes

- Map the location of the genes

- Create a data bank of detailed information about the structure, organization, and function of human DNA

- Give the information discovered to any scientist, doctor, or other researcher who can use it

- Continue to examine the ethical, legal, and social issues arising from human genetics research and develop policy options for public consideration

- Train scientists to use the technologies developed through the project, in order to improve human health[3]

The Human Genome Project is the most organized, well-financed, and ambitious plan ever developed to study genes. Scientists did not have to wait until the project was finished to take advantage of the information collected, said Dr. Francis Collins, director of the National Human Genome Research Institute. "Working draft data, as soon as it becomes publicly available, is very helpful to scientists today in their efforts to understand the hereditary influences on health and disease and to develop more targeted diagnosis and treatment procedures."[4]

The first phase of the project—the working draft of the human genome—was on track for spring 2000. The next phase of the project focused on producing a complete, accurate gene sequence by the year 2003 or before, but it, too, was finished in 2000. The data published by the project provided a basic reference that will keep work from being duplicated as other researchers pursue answers to genetics questions. Some experts said that the finished project should allow scientists to simply pull out the DNA for a specific gene on a chromosome for study, therapy, or removal. In fact, possible uses for the information are far-reaching. Responsible scientists also caution that the information should be used carefully.

President Bill Clinton's State of the Union Address on January 27, 1999, referred often to genetics research and the Human Genome Project. He said:

> In the new century, innovations in science and technology will be the key not only to the health of the environment, but to miraculous improvements in the quality of our lives. . . . Later this year, researchers will complete the first draft of the entire human genome, the very blueprint of life. It is important for all our fellow Americans to recognize that federal tax dollars have funded much of this research, and that this and other wise investments in science are leading to a revolution in our ability to detect, treat, and prevent disease.

The president also summarized research in gene therapy: "For example, researchers have identified genes that cause Parkinson's, diabetes, and certain kinds of cancer—they are [designing] precision therapies that will block the harmful effect of these genes for good."

While President Clinton praised biotechnology advances, he also cautioned that privacy and ethics should be maintained. "Now, these new breakthroughs have to be used in ways that reflect our values. First and foremost, we have to safeguard our citizens' privacy. Last year, we proposed to protect every citizen's medical record. This year, we will finalize those rules. . . . We must also act to prevent any genetic discrimination whatever by employers or insurers."

In his final remarks on the subject, President Clinton was perhaps warning us not to pursue a course in genetic engineering that would lead to perfect babies for every couple. "Modern science has confirmed what ancient faiths have always taught," he said, "the most important fact of life is our common humanity. Therefore, we should do more than just tolerate our diversity—we should honor it and celebrate it."[5]

Coming Soon to a Laboratory Near You

In the book *The Biotech Century*, author Jeremy Rifkin recites a long list of possibilities as genetics research progresses. Over the next ten to twenty years:

- Farming may move indoors, because most food products will be grown in tissue cultures, saving farmers both time and money.

- New hybrid plant species will be developed. Some will have the ability to grow in colder temperatures or to stay fresh on grocery shelves longer. Others will taste better or be good for our health.

- New animal species could appear, to be used as organ donors, or to produce hormones and other substances for human benefit. Animal and human cloning could be common, with reproduction as we know it giving way to replication (cloning).

- People can obtain their own genetic blueprints to look into their own futures or to find suitable mates.[6]

Again, many argue that the above changes may not be all good. New animal and plant species could take over, crowding out some of the species we now know. This could lead to less diversity among living things, which is difficult enough to preserve without genetic engineering. Genetic blueprints of ourselves could lead to decisions too difficult to contemplate. And many prospective parents will still want to let nature take its course, instead of "designing" perfect babies.

As genetic research progresses, some predict that farming will move indoors. Gone will be the colorful agricultural fields of yesteryear—and today.

Has the Future Arrived?

Some say that the future of biotechnology is now. For instance, biochips would have been difficult to predict just a few years ago. Biochips are small pieces of glass containing genes that interact in certain ways with the DNA of any tissue placed on them. In a process similar to etching silicon microchips for computers, thousands of fragments of DNA are layered onto a piece of glass.

The DNA used in biochips is specific to tests being conducted. For example, to test for drug-resistant tuberculosis (TB), researchers combine two DNA solutions. One solution contains drug-resistant TB DNA. The other contains DNA from the sputum of a patient being tested. Scientists then look for bonding of base pairs—adenine, cytosine, thymine, and guanine. A fluorescent dye is added to the biochip, which seeks out base pairs. Bases on the chip that have paired with bases from a patient sample light up. The stronger the light, the stronger the bond. A computer designed to read the biochips quickly converts the light to data. The test can confirm whether or not a patient has a drug-resistant form of TB.

The chips allow users to conduct thousands of different medical tests at once, in a short period of time. Biochips are in development that can be used to find TB infection and identify the specific strain of bacteria responsible for the infection. In 1999, drug-resistant tuberculosis was selected as a demonstration for the technology because infection has become widespread worldwide. Over the past twenty

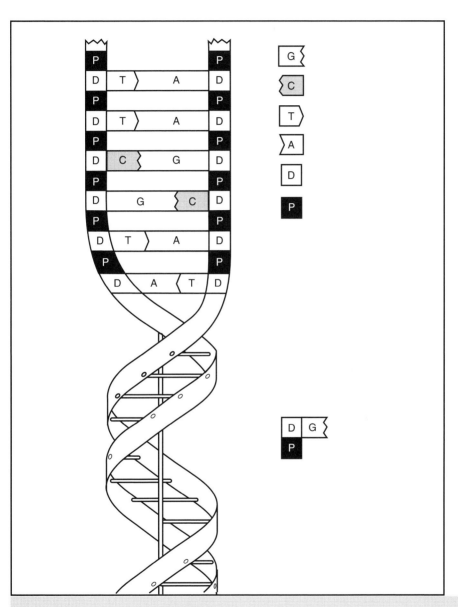

The key to genetic engineering is the way in which DNA is combined and recombined.

years, strains of mutated tuberculosis bacteria have developed that are immune to the most common antibiotics used to treat the infection. Biochips could be the fastest and most effective way of diagnosing the drug-resistant strains of TB bacteria. This would allow doctors to quickly tell which antibiotics will kill the organism.

Biochip technology is also in use to discover new drugs that can cure various diseases. For instance, a chip was developed to show whether or not a certain breast cancer mutation could be treated with the drug Herceptin.

Biochips are also being developed that can detect genetically engineered organisms used in war or terrorism attacks.[7]

Here are a few other developments in genetic research reported at the beginning of the twenty-first century:

- Researchers created the first laboratory-grown human corneas. The bioengineered tissue could replace some chemical testing on animal eyes. It was also a major step toward creating artificial corneas for human transplant.[8]

- An American company developed a salve that, when rubbed on a balding scalp, can transfer a functional gene into the hair follicles. If the company's search for hair growth factor genes is successful, hair loss replacement is possible. The treatment might be used for the hair loss that occurs in cancer chemotherapy treatments.[9]

- Italian geneticists isolated a gene in mice linked to many of the ill effects of aging. The gene has been found to release a protein that destroys cells damaged by oxygen, a process believed to prevent cancerous cells from forming. Cell death over time leads to a general breakdown of the body and such symptoms of aging as wrinkles and gray hair. Mice genetically engineered not to produce the protein lived 30 percent longer than normal mice, with no noticeable side effects. Researchers believe the same gene could be blocked in humans, perhaps with the same result.[10]

Potential Risks

As genetics research continues to progress, scientists and ethicists caution that we must consider possible side effects, as well as benefits. Answers to these questions and more will be needed in the years ahead:

- If farmers are no longer needed to grow food, what will the millions of farmers do to earn a living? And what will happen to national economies, worldwide, when agricultural workers are displaced? Of course, during the course of history, the displaced worker question has been raised before. Economies have adjusted to changes in the workplace, to accommodate seamstresses put out of work by sewing machines, blacksmiths displaced by the automobile, assembly-line workers replaced by robots, and so on.

- What will be the long-term effect if we release millions of new plant and animal species into the environment? Will we so disturb the balance of nature that it can never recover?

- Will the human race be truly improved if every disorder and imperfection is forever removed from the gene pool?

- How will religious beliefs hold up when it seems that humans can now play God?

- Will we create new social classes through genetic engineering? In the 1997 movie *Gattaca*, such a story is played out. Only the genetically enhanced can hold the best jobs. "Love children" produced by natural means are the workers and have little chance to better themselves. The hero of the story is of the "natural" class and cannot be a space explorer because of a genetic heart condition.

Caution Urged by Responsible Scientists

In the future, answers to the above questions will be important. Responsible scientists say the answers lie in caution. While we rush to reap the benefits of new genetic technology, we must not ignore the downside. The answer for those of us who may benefit from genetic research successes, or suffer from failures, is to learn all we can about a new bioengineered food, drug, treatment, or process before drawing conclusions. The biotechnology policy statement of the Union of Concerned Scientists (UCS) perhaps says it best:

UCS has no fundamental objection to genetic engineering or any other form of biotechnology. For example, moving genes across species lines does not, in our view, violate any principle so important as to override use of this technology for beneficial purposes . . .

[W]e weigh the benefits of the technology against its risks, and if the benefits are sufficient, we welcome the application. In addition, we always try to consider alternative methods of achieving purported benefits.

Consequently, we do not think that genetic engineering must be accepted or rejected as a whole, and we consider each application individually. We believe that society can welcome some applications and not others.

The key to understanding and adapting to advances in genetics, reminds the UCS, is to "reject both extremes in the biotechnology debate . . ."[11]

In short, we should ask the hard questions about all forms of genetics research. Then we can form opinions that are subject to change as new evidence comes to light. We should not fear and condemn the technology as unnatural before we have considered the pros and cons. By the same token, we should not embrace every new development before proof is in about risks and benefits.

Chapter Notes

Chapter 1. Welcome to the Clone Age

1. Associated Press, "Dolly Had Three Little Lambs," April 1, 1999, <http://www.abcnews.go.com/sections/science/DailyNews/cloning_dolly990401.html> (November 1, 1999).

2. Emma Ross, "How Close Are We to Cloning Ourselves?" *Rapid City Journal*, August 15, 2000, p. C3.

3. Public Broadcasting System, Newshour Transcript, February 24, 1997, <http://www1.pbs.org/newshour/bb/science/jan-june97/cloning_2-24.html> (November 2, 1999).

4. Animal Cloning Abstracts, *AgBiotech News & Information (ANI)*, March, 1998, <http://www.cabi.org/whatsnew/cloneani.htm> (November 1, 1999).

5. Ibid.

6. Tim Friend, "Britain Endorses Cloning Human Embryos," *USA Today*, August 17, 2000, p. 1A.

7. "Executive Summary—Cloning Human Beings," n.d., <http://bioethics.gov/pubs/cloning1/executive.htm> (May 23, 2000).

8. Irene Stith-Coleman, "Cloning: Where Do We Go From Here?" *CRS Report for Congress*, January 2000, <http://www.pub.umich.edu/daily/1998/jan/01-16-98/edit/edit2.html> (August 21, 2000).

9. CNN Interactive, January 7, 1998, audio version of interview, <http://www.cnn.com/TECH/9801/07/cloning.folo/index.html> (November 2, 1999).

10. Animal Cloning Abstracts.

11. "Welcome to the Clone Age," n.d., <http://www.teleport.com/~samc/clone> (November 1, 1999).

12. MSNBC staff and wire reports, "Is Cloning Key to Fountain of Youth?" n.d., <wysiwyg://36http://www.msnbc.com/news/400436.asp?cp1=1> (May 23, 2000).

13. Ibid.

14. "Cloning Special Report," *New Scientist*, n.d., <http://www.nsplus.com/nsplus/insight/clone/faq.html> (November 1, 1999).

15. Glenn McGee, *The Human Cloning Debate* (Berkeley, Calif.: Berkeley Hills Books, 1998), pp. 27–28.

16. D.M. Potts and W.T.W. Potts, *Queen Victoria's Gene,* n.d., <http://www.adamandeve.net/queenmain.htm> (December 10, 1999).

17. Maya Pines, "Why so Many Errors in Our DNA?" *Blazing a Genetic Trail*, n.d., <http://www.bioeducation.org/genetictrail/errors/wyso.htm> (December 16, 1999).

Chapter 2. Genetic Engineering

1. James Patterson, *When The Wind Blows* (New York: Warner Books), 1998.

2. Fred Warshofsky, "The Methuselah Factor," *Modern Maturity*, November-December 1999, pp. 28–32, 76.

3. "Genetically Modified Food (GMF)," Government of New Zealand, n.d., <http://www.maf.govt.nz/MAFnet/schools/activities/gmfbio.htm.P.6> (May 26, 2000).

4. *The Washington Post*, "Bio-Rice Called Nutrition, P.R. Booster," reprinted in *Rapid City Journal*, January 14, 2000, p. A5.

5. Phil Lempert, "The Next Big Thing in Food: Choices," *USA Weekend,* November 12-14, 1999, pp. 7–10.

6. "Fear and Ignorance and Biotech," *Chicago Tribune*, January 31, 2000, <wysiwyg://4/http://chicagotribune.com/ne...on/article/0,2669,SAV-0001310003,FF.html> (January 31, 2000).

7. "Genetically Modified Food," p. 6.

8. James Cox, "Bio-Crops Under Attack," *USA Today*, January 31, 2000, 1B-2B.

9. "Genetically Modified Food," p. 8.

10. Ibid., p. 9.

11. Doug Palmer, "Countries Reach Landmark GMO Food Agreement," *World Headlines*, January 29, 2000, <http://dailynews.yahoo.com/h/nm/20000129/wl/food_un_3.html> (February 1, 2000).

12. Nell Boyce, "Monster Protest Against Frankenscience," *New Scientist*, November 6, 1999, p. 12.

13. Geoffrey Cowley, "A Pig May Someday Save Your Life," *Newsweek*, January 1, 2000, p. 88.

14. Ibid., p. 87.

15. Ibid.

16. Warshofsky, p. 32.

17. Ibid.

18. Martin Kettle, "Scientists Spin DNA Into Super Material," *Rapid City Journal*, May 22, 2000, p. A1, reprinted from *The Guardian*.

19. Kathleen Fackelmann, "Engineered Corn Kills Butterflies, Study Says," *USA Today*, May 20, 1999, p. 1A.

20. Rick Weiss, "Gene-Altered Corn's Impact Reassessed," *Washington Post*, November 3, 1999, p. A3.

21. Dr. W. French Anderson, "A Cure That May Cost Us Ourselves," *Newsweek*, January 1, 2000, pp. 75–76.

Chapter 3. Gene Therapy

1. Rita Rubin, "Medical Advances Help to Eliminate Tragic 'Bubble Boy' Syndrome," *USA Today*, as reprinted in online edition of *Detroit News*, February 20, 1999, <http://detroitnews.com/1999/health/9902/20/02200067.htm> (May 22, 2000).

2. The David Vetter Website, "David's Dream," n.d., <http://www.meteorweb.com/davidsdream/davidsdream.html> (May 22, 2000).

3. Tim Friend, "Genetic Disease Responds to Gene Therapy," *USA Today*, 4/28–30/00, p. 4A.

4. The Associated Press, "Tighter Tracking Urged for Gene Trials," *USA Today*, December 13, 1999, p. 10D.

5. Paul Recer, Associated Press, "Accusations in Gene Therapy Death," *Yahoo! News, Science Headlines*, February 3, 2000, <http://dailynews.yahoo.com/htx/ap/20000203/sc/gene_therapy_teen_4.html> (February 3, 2000).

6. Ibid.

7. Abbey S. Meyers, "A Look At . . . Informed Consent," *Washington Post*, January 30, 2000, p. B3.

8. Ibid.

9. Philip Kitcher, *The Lives to Come: The Genetic Revolution and Human Possibilities* (New York: Simon & Schuster, 1996), pp. 114-117.

Chapter 4. Genetic Testing

1. "Facts About Cystic Fibrosis," Cystic Fibrosis Foundation, n.d., <http://cff.org/facts.htm> (February 14, 2000).

2. Maya Pines, "A Gifted Young Patient Seeks His Own Genetic Flaw," *Blazing a Genetic Trail: Stalking a Lethal Gene*, n.d., <http://www.bioeducation.org/genetictrail/stalking/gift.htm> (December 16, 1999).

3. Ibid.

4. Ruth Hubbard and Elijah Wald, *Exploding the Gene Myth* (Boston: Beacon Press, 1993), p. 35.

5. Geoffrey Cowley and Anne Underwood, "A Revolution in Medicine," *Newsweek*, April 10, 2000, p. 58.

6. Ibid.

7. Maya Pines, "Who Should Be Tested? Screening for CF and Other Genetic Diseases," *Blazing a Genetic Trail: Research on Mutant Genes and Hereditary Diseases*, n.d., <http://www.bioeducation.org/genetictrail/stalking/who.htm> (December 16, 1999).

8. Jeremy Rifkin, *The Biotech Century* (New York: Jeremy P. Tarcher/Putnam, 1998), pp. 134–135.

9. Edward Connors et. al., "Convicted by Juries, Exonerated by Science," Criminal Lawyers' Association, August 1996, <http://www.ncjrs.org/txtfiles/dnaevid.txt> (May 30, 2000).

10. Bob Herbert, "How Many Innocent Prisoners?" *The New York Times*, July 18, 1999, <http://www.truthinjustice.org/vincentjenkins.htm> (May 30, 2000).

11. Ibid.

12. "Innocence Project at Cardozo," Cardozo School of Law, n.d., <http://www.cardozo.yu.edu/innocence_project/index.html> (May 31, 2000).

13. "Genetic Testing May Fight Organ Rejection," *USA Today*, May 15, 2000, p. 5D.

14. Associated Press, "Group Wants Families to Keep DNA Documented," May 29, 2000, p. A2.

Chapter 5. Genetic Discrimination, Privacy, and Civil Liberties

1. Tim Friend, "Researchers Uncover Genetic Discrimination," *USA Today*, April 12, 1996, p.3A, <http://www.usatoday.com/life/health/lhs461.htm> (May 31, 2000).

2. Ibid.

3. Sharon Begley, "Decoding the Human Body," *Newsweek*, April 10, 2000, p. 56.

4. Friend.

5. Begley.

6. Friend.

7. Begley.

8. Laurence McQuillan, "Clinton Restricts Use of Genetic Data," *USA Today*, February 9, 2000, p. 15A.

9. *The Arc: A Report on The Arc's Human Genome Education Project*, vol. 1. no. 2.4, "Genetic Issues In Mental Retardation," n.d., <http://thearc.org/depts/gbr02.html> (February 18, 2000).

10. Lisa N. Geller, J.S. Alper, P.R. Billings, C.I. Barash, J. Beckwith, and M. Natowicz, "Individual, Family, and Societal Dimensions of Genetic Discrimination: A Case Study Analysis," *Science and Engineering Ethics*, vol. 2, issue 1, January 1996, pp. 71–88.

11. Ibid.

12. Jeremy Rifkin, The Biotech Century (New York: Jeremy P. Tarcher/Putnam, 1998), p. 163.

13. Ruth Hubbard and Elijah Wald, *Exploding the Gene Myth* (Boston: Beacon Press, 1993), p. 135.

14. Rifkin, p. 164.

15. Ibid.

16. Maya Pines, "Who Should Be Tested? Screening for CF and Other Genetic Diseases," *Blazing a Genetic Trail: Research on Mutant Genes and Hereditary Diseases*, <http://www.bioeducation.org/genetictrail/stalking/who.htm> (December 16,1999).

17. Hubbard and Wald, p. 129.

18. Geller, et. al., p. 78.

19. Rifkin, pp. 117–119.

Chapter 6. The Gene Business

1. Tim Friend, "It's In The Genes: Scientists Confront Money Issues," *USA Today*, February 22, 2000, p. 7D.

2. Ibid.

3. Adam Bryant, "The Gold Rush," *Newsweek*, April 10, 2000, p. 67.

4. Friend.

5. Ruth Hubbard and Elijah Wald, *Exploding the Gene Myth* (Boston: Beacon Press, 1993), p. 119.

6. Jeremy Rifkin, *The Biotech Century* (New York: Jeremy P. Tarcher/Penguin, 1998), pp. 60–61.

7. Ibid., p. 141.

8. Andrew Kimbrell, *The Human Body Shop: The Engineering and Marketing of Life* (San Francisco: Harper, 1993), pp. 142–144.

9. Rick Boling, "A Shot of Youth," *Modern Maturity*, March-April 2000, p. 70.

10. Werth, Barry, "How Short Is Too Short?" *The New York Times* magazine, June 16, 1991, p. 15.

11. Hubbard and Wald, p. 69.

12. Boling, p. 71.

13. Ibid.

14. Ibid.

15. Robin Mather, *A Garden of Unearthly Delights: Bioengineering and the Future of Food* (New York: Dutton, 1995), p. 13.

16. Rifkin, pp. 41–43.

17. Ibid., p. 44.

18. Friend.

19. Tara Weingarten and Mark Hosenball, "A Fertile Scheme," *Newsweek*, November 8, 1999, pp. 78–79.

20. Carey Goldberg, "On Web, Models Auction Their Eggs to Bidders for Beautiful Children," *The New York Times*, October 23, 1999, p. A11.

Chapter 7. Genetics in Our Future

1. Matt Crenson, "After a Decade Cataloging Human Genes, Scientists Begin the Hard Part," *Associated Press*, May 27, 2000.

2. Jean-Michel Claverie, "What If There Are Only 30,000 Human Genes?" *Science*, vol. 291, no. 5507, February 16, 2001, pp. 1255–1257.

3. "The Human Genome Project," *National Institutes of Health*, n.d., <http://www.nhgri.nih.gov/HCP> (November 1, 1999).

4. "Human Genome Will Be Defined by Spring," *National Human Genome Research Institute*, n.d. <http://www.nhgri.nih.gov/NEWS/human_genome_defined_by_spring.html> (February 25, 2000).

5. "President's State of the Union Address Refers to Human Genome Project," *National Human Genome Research Institute*, January 27, 1999, <http://www.nhgri.nih.gov/NEWS/president.html> (February 25, 2000).

6. Jeremy Rifkin, *The Biotech Century* (New York: Jeremy P. Tarcher/Penguin, 1998), p. 3.

7. Tim Friend, "A Tactic Against Tuberculosis," *USA Today*, October 18, 1999, p. 4D.

8. Olivia Barker, "Corneas Grown in Lab," *USA Today*, December 13, 1999, p. 10D.

9. Dr. W. French Anderson, "A Cure That May Cost Us Ourselves," *Newsweek*, January 1, 2000, p. 76.

10. Michael Eskenazi, "He's An Old Mouse, But Spry. Are We Next?" *Time Inc.* New Media, November 18, 1999, <http://www.pathfinder.com/time/daily/0,2960,34641-101990008,00.html> (December 10, 1999).

11. "Biotechnology Positions," *Union of Concerned Scientists*, n.d., <http://www.ucsusa.org/news/posbiotech.html> (February 25, 2000).

Further Reading

Hawkes, Nigel. *Genetic Engineering*. New York: Franklin Watts, Inc., 1991.

Hooper, Tony. *Breakthrough: Genetics*. Austin, Tex.: Raintree Steck-Vaughn Publishers, 1994.

Kilata, Gina. Clone: *The Road To Dolly and the Path Ahead*. New York: William Morrow and Company, 1998.

Kimbrell, Andrew. *The Human Body Shop: The Engineering and Marketing of Life*. New York: HarperCollins, 1993.

Mather, Robin. *Garden of Unearthly Delights: Bioengineering and the Future of Food*. New York: Dutton, 1995.

McCuen, Gary E. *Cloning, Science & Society*. Hudson, Wisc.: McCuen Publications, Inc., 1998.

Pence, Gregory E. *Who's Afraid of Human Cloning?* New York: Rowman & Littlefield Publishers, Inc., 1998.

Rifkin, Jeremy. *The Biotech Century*. New York: Jeremy P. Tarcher/Putnam, 1998.

Roleff, Tamara L., ed. *Biomedical Ethics: Opposing Viewpoints*. San Diego, Calif.: Greenhaven Press, Inc., 1998.

Wekesser, Carol, ed. *Genetic Engineering: Opposing Viewpoints*. San Diego, Calif.: Greenhaven Press, Inc., 1996.

Zallen, Doris Teichler. *Does It Run in the Family? A Consumer's Guide to DNA Testing for Genetic Disorders*. New Brunswick, N.J.: Rutgers University Press, 1997.

Internet Addresses

Information about various aspects of genetics and genetics testing:

"Blazing a Genetic Trail," Howard Hughes Medical Institute
<http://www.hhmi.org/genetictrail/index.html>

General genetics information:

Genetic Science Learning Center
<http://gslc.genetics.utah.edu>

<http://www.genetics.about.com>

Information about the *National Human Genome Research Institute*:

<http://www.genome.gov>

Information about all aspects of the Human Genome Project, *National Institutes of Health*:

<http://www.genome.gov/page.cfm?pageID= 10001694>

Information about genetics research:

Institute for Genomic Research
<http://www.tigr.org>

Information about human cloning:

<http://www.humancloning.org>

Glossary

albinism—The absence of pigment in plants and animals, caused by a gene mutation.

biochips—Pieces of glass containing genes that interact in certain ways with the DNA of any tissue placed on them.

biotechnology—Another term for genetic engineering and recombinant DNA technology.

chromosome—A structure found inside the nuclei of human cells that replicates itself, in order to pass on genes responsible for hereditary traits.

clone—An exact replica of an organism, produced by one parent cell, instead of by union of egg and sperm.

cytoplasm—The jelly-like substance that comprises plant and animal cells.

deoxyribonucleic acid (DNA)—The living tissue, made up of nucleotides, that comprises chromosomes.

dominant—Refers to genes responsible for traits that are almost always expressed if the gene is present; in a gene pair, prevents the recessive trait from being expressed.

double helix—The twisted shape of the DNA molecule.

eugenics—The science that deals with the improvement of inherited characteristics in a race or species.

gametes—Egg and sperm cells.

gene—A self-producing unit located on a chromosome; responsible for an organism's traits.

gene therapy—Involves inserting genes into human embryos or other body tissue to correct or prevent diseases.

genetic engineering—The process of splicing genetic material from plants, animals, or bacteria into the DNA of other organisms.

genetics—The branch of biology that deals with the study of heredity (how traits are inherited) and variations among organisms.

genome—All of an organism's genetic information.

genotype—An organism's genetic makeup.

hemophilia—An inherited blood disorder in which blood does not clot normally, due to the lack of one or more factors responsible for the clotting of blood.

heredity—An organism's pattern of inheritance.

Human Genome Project—An international scientific project to locate all the genes on the twenty-three pairs of human chromosomes.

in vitro—Latin for "in glass," as when eggs are fertilized in a test tube, outside of a woman's body.

meiosis—Cell division that produces eggs and sperm.

Mendel, Gregor—A Czech monk who grew pea plants to study heredity; called the father of modern genetics.

mitosis—Cell division of all body cells except egg and sperm cells.

mutagens—Agents that cause mutations.

mutation—A change that occurs in a chromosome's DNA during replication.

nuclear transfer—A cloning technique that involves fusing a donor cell with an unfertilized egg that has had its nucleus removed.

nucleus—The dense inner structure of genetic material inside every plant and animal cell.

patent—The legal right to an invention or product, giving the creator exclusive rights to sell or license his or her invention.

ratio—Fixed pattern of events.

recessive—Refers to genes responsible for traits expressed only if the dominant gene is not present.

recombinant DNA—The term for the DNA formed by splicing together the DNA from different organisms.

sex cells—Specialized cells responsible for reproduction in plants and animals.

sex chromosomes—One pair of chromosomes that determines the sex of the individual. In humans, two X chromosomes produce a female and an XY combination produces a male.

sex-linked traits—Genes for these traits are carried on the X chromosome.

trait—Characteristic of a plant or animal, such as height, weight, color.

Index

A

ADA deficiency, 47
aging, 37–38, 92, 109
Alzado, Lyle, 91–92
American Medical
    Association (AMA), 87,
    88
Americans With Disabilities
    Act (ADA), 73, 75
Anderson, W. French, 41–42
Annas, George, 72

B

Baltimore, David, 86
biochips, 106, 108
biotechnology, 25
    agricultural, 30–33
    animal, 33–34
    old and new, 27–30
    bovine growth hormone
    (BGH), 51, 52
Bt corn, 39, 40
Bubble Boy, 47
Burbank, Luther, 81

C

Caplan, Arthur, 98, 99
carriers, 53
Chakrabarty, Ananda,
    94–95
chromosomes, 9, 16, 18,
    19, 100
    sex-determining, 45
Clinton, Bill, 11, 73, 74,
    103–104
cloning, 7–16
Code of Medical Ethics, 87,
    88

Collins, Francis, 102
Common Rule, 49–50
Coolidge, Calvin, 81, 82
Council for Responsible
    Genetics, 88
Council of Europe, 10
curse of the Coburgs, 43–44
cystic fibrosis, 47, 55–58,
    66

D

Davenport, Charles, 81
DNA, 16–18, 23, 24–25,
    41, 53–54, 100, 101,
    107
    goat, 38
    spider, 38
    testing, 66–69
Dolly, 7–8, 19, 24
Down syndrome, 59
dwarfism, 52, 90–91

E

Equal Employment
    Opportunities
    Commission, 73
eugenics, 81–83
European corn borer, 39
Exploding the Gene Myth,
    78

F

Factor VIII, 52
Fano, Alix, 34
Federal Drug
    Administration, 90–91
fragile X disease, 59, 60,
    62–63

free radicals, 37–38
fruit flies, 29, 37

G

Galton, Francis, 81
Gaucher's disease, 59, 77
Geller, Lisa N., 75, 76, 77, 79
Gelsinger, Jesse, 48, 49, 96
gene therapy, 43–54
  germ line, 47
  somatic cell, 45
genes, 9, 23, 101
genetic discrimination, 71–79
genetic diseases, likelihood of developing, 63
genetic engineering, 24–25, 27–42
  drugs and hormones, 51–52
genetic material, 16–19
  inheritance of, 18, 19
genetic testing, 55–70
  ethical, legal, and social issues in, 69–70, 80–81, 83
  process, 64
  who should be tested, 64–67
Genewatch, 88

H

Harriman, Mrs. E. H., 81
Harris, Ron, 99
Health Insurance Portability and Accountability Act (HIPAA), 73
hemochromatosis, 58, 60, 61, 75
hemophilia, 44–45, 47, 52, 62
heredity, 25
HIV, 47

Hospital Necker-Enfants Malades, 48
Hubbard, Ruth, 78
Human Genome Project, 100–104
human growth hormone (HGH), 51–52, 90–94
human insulin, 51, 52
Huntington's disease, 59, 60–63, 71–72, 75, 76

I

immune system, 36, 47, 48
informed consent, 49
Innocence Project, 67–68
institutional review boards (IRBs), 50
in vitro fertilization (IVF), 66

J

Jenkins, Vincent, 67
Jordan, David Starr, 81

K

Kellogg, J.H., 81

L

Lantos, John D., 92
Lanza, Robert P., 14

M

Medical Information Bureau, 79
Melias, Robert, 67
Mendel, Gregor, 19–23, 28
Mintz, Alan, 92
monarch caterpillars (butterflies), 39–40
Moore, John, 89. 90
Morelli, Theresa, 71–72
mucopolysaccaridosis (MPS), 75, 76
muscular dystrophy, 47
mutations, 23–24

N

National Bioethics Advisory Committee, 11
National Human Genome Research Institute, 102
National Institutes of Health, 49, 86, 87, 100, 101
National Research Act of 1974, 50
Neufeld, Peter, 67
New Scientist, 15
nuclear transfer, 9
nucleotides, 16, 17

O

Olson, Maynard V., 87
ornithine transcarbamylase deficiency (OTC), 48

P

Patterson, James, 27
Pennington, Robert, 36, 37
phenylketonuria (PKU), 59, 75
pigs, genetically altered, 36, 37
Pinard, Jeff, 55–56, 58
Pleasant, John, 40
Prince Leopold, Duke of Albany, 44
privacy issues, 79–80
Project LifePrint, 68–69

Q

Queen Victoria, 43–46

R

rheumotoid arthritis, 47
Rifkin, Jeremy, 104
Rissler, Jane, 40
Rose, Michael, 29
Roslin Institute, 7, 9

S

Schechter, Alan, 86
Scheck, Barry, 67
Schon, Eric, 8
Seargent, Terri, 72
Seed, Richard, 11–12
selective breeding, 28-30
severe combined immune deficiency (SCID), 47, 48, 54
sickle-cell anemia, 59, 77–78
Skirboll, Lana, 87
Smith, Shelley, 99
spinocerebellar ataxia, 59
Sohal, Raj, 37
stem cells, 12–13
Stephenson, Jamie, 71

T

Tay-Sachs disease, 59
transgenics, 34
Tseng, Scheffer, 88–89
Turner, Jeffrey, 38

U

Union of Concerned Scientists, 40, 110, 111
United States Patent and Trademark Office (PTO), 94, 95, 96

V

Vetter, David, 47

W

Wald, Elijah, 78
When The Wind Blows, 27
World War II, 49

X

xenotransplantation, 34–36, 38